GRACE&
SPEED

JOHN B. OLABODE

Unless otherwise indicated, all Scripture quotations are taken from the King James Version of the Bible.

GRACE & SPEED

ISBN: 978-978-57898-8-1

Copyright © 2020
John B. Olabode

Published by
Gihon Spring Trans-National Ltd
Block C, Adebowale House, Onipanu, Lagos.
Tel: +234 (0) 803 620 7471, 809 820 7471
E-mail: gihonprinters@gmail.com
info@gihonpublications.com
www.gihonpublications.com

Printed in Nigeria.

CONTENTS

PREFACE

THE LIFE WE LIVE IS a function of God's grace, the Bible says 'the race is not to the swift, the battle is not to the strong but time and chance happens to them all'.

Grace is the God–factor in the race of life, the book of John 15 says without Him, we can do nothing. Life is very much about God, as many as appear before God in Zion go from strength to strength. Going through life without understanding places a man on a disadvantaged path.

The book is about understanding the God–factor in our lives and how to properly connect to God. The chapters of the book showcase the need to see and connect to God in all aspects of life. The book also teaches about the basic necessities on how to maximize God's grace to achieve full potential. Many in the Christendom have assumed that with 'Grace', you just go and sleep while Grace works even when you are doing nothing.

Grace doesn't make a lazy man rather it places demand on us the more about the need to fully utilize what has been made available for us. Hear the voice of the apostle Paul in one of his epistles, 'I am what I am by the grace of God nevertheless I work harder than any other person.'

This book is a must for all who intend to fully utilize the grace of God in their lives.

ACKNOWLEDGMENT

ALL GLORY TO THE ALMIGHTY God and His Spirit that has birthed this great inspiration.

I would like to thank my Father in the Lord, Apostle Martins Atanda, Uncle Bayo Famonure and their families for their fatherly counsel and encouragement through these years. To all the assistant pastors in King's Assembly; Pastor Abdul, Matawal, Osunbor, Chima, Tunde, Mrs. Ogbara, Raymond and Rev. Okoro. To all the PFN Sokoto State Chapter executives; Pastor Ben, Pastor Fred, Pastor Kato, Pastor Benedict and Pastor Dr. Uche, I appreciate your support.

I would also like to appreciate my beautiful wife, Vera for her unending support and prayers. Thanks to my children Tola, Emmanuel and Anna for bearing with my busy schedule. All my siblings (Mrs. Olagunju, Wale, Yemi, Ayo, and Niyi) and my several spiritual children all over the world have been wonderful.

To all the departmental leaders in the church, Ushers (Mrs Lola Olumoh), Protocols (Mrs. Uche Philo), Streaming (Miss Yemisi), Church Secretary (Mrs. Funmi Ogunlaja), Choir (Pastor Chima), Media (Mr. Ibukun), Finance (Mrs. Edayi Eniola), Technical (Bro Matthew), Managers (Mr. Debo, Mrs. Peterside and Dr. Susan), Youth (Dr. Susan and Mr. Abraham), King's Women (Mrs. Naomi Waziri, Mrs. Momoh and Pastor Vera), King's Men (Prof. Momoh and Mr. Odibo), Decoration (Mrs. Osunbor), Children department (Pastor (Mrs.) Vera and Mrs. Helen Adejoh), I say a very big thank you.

Also, appreciation goes to everyone who contributed to the production of this book, Obadiah Oyetoro, the Chief Editor, Victoria Olawole and Oluwafemi Irene for making sure all the logistics involved in publishing this book were handled in a professional and timely manner.

DEDICATION

I DEDICATE THIS BOOK TO the Holy Spirit, my greatest inspiration and to my late parents for raising me up in the way of the Lord in my early days.

1

KINGDOM SERVICE

'Then Peter began to say unto him, Lo, we have left all, and have followed thee. And Jesus answered and said, Verily I say unto you, There is no man that hath left house, or brethren, or sisters, or father, or mother, or wife, or children, or lands, for my sake, and the gospel's, But he shall receive an hundredfold now in this time, houses, and brethren, and sisters, and mothers, and children, and lands, with persecutions; and in the world to come eternal life.' Mark 10:28–30 (KJV)

THERE ARE ALL KINDS OF services but all service should be tied to the kingdom. The purpose of every service should end in the kingdom. You must find an area you can serve and focus on Jesus. For every child of God to be protected, you have to be involved in kingdom service; serve with your whole might. If you are useful in the house of God, do you think God will watch death do away with you? There are people in the house of God who play very vital role(s), their absence creates a gap that takes a long time to fill, hence, God is also committed to his word. After salvation, do you want to sit down waiting for the kingdom of God when it is said that the kingdom of heaven is with you? That's why you must find a place to serve and pour your heart into it.

It is great ignorance to assume that everyone likes you because they laugh with you. There might be people laughing with you yet they hate you. However, they can't do you anything as long as you are committed to serving God. I am showing you the power to security and success in life as you get involved in kingdom service, this is why you don't promote your name or engage in self-service other than kingdom service.

Kingdom service makes God committed to your deliverance. If you are not serving, you will spend all your life binding demons. The time expended on binding demons can be dedicated to serving God, then the demons are taking care of by God's angels. That's why Jesus will look at demons and rebuke them. There was no demon Jesus spent all night forbidding, he wouldn't spend all night because he had work to do (John 9:4). Kingdom service is a priority, else, you are held back and you are gone! I advise people not to be bench-warmers in church. Somebody sometimes told me, 'I just want to come quietly and go quietly', that is how people have come quietly to church and gone quietly to their graves. You must choose to get actively involved in kingdom service wherever God has placed you (Ecclesiastes 9:10).

Service as a Sunday school teacher

Several years ago, I was a Sunday school teacher–that was my job; there was so much joy in serving. I was teaching young children and I did a lot of illustrations. I had the understanding that you can't teach children, using iPad and ask them what they have learnt after teaching. They would reply 'microphone' because your appearance was a distraction, that's where I started my ministry, always dancing and praising God with children.

As a children evangelist, teaching children was something I loved so much. When people were in the main church, I was never for once moved to go to adult church to handle microphone and lead the service. Even when the church organized major conferences that had over five hundred (500) children present, I was placed in charge of the children, praying for them and fasting with them. Today, some of those children have grown into adults, some have become mothers. I was happy serving without raising any complaint about what I have been asked to do. Today, when I teach children, other people enjoy and love what I do.

Remember that it was a delight that was my portion and I did it well. I did that till I went for my national service year while I was still engaged in other programs that had to involve my presence. Serving the children was my assignment and as I served God in this capacity, He kept me alive to keep praying and fasting for protection. Expend the time you use for fasting to serve God; find a place that he is leading you and pour your heart there in service to God in holiness and righteousness all the days of your life without rivalry or strife. You may think that place where you are serving God is not really important; that is not true. His parameters for reward is different.

Find a place and pour your heart to what God has assigned you to do for every season; every assignment has a season. To be a cleaner in the house of God murmuring, *they think I can't lead prayer, let them give me the microphone and see what I will do. I will scatter the place'* is the reason why the microphone didn't get to you at first because you are scattered. Is your portion to sweep? Do it well!

God still rewards faithful men

There was a time when my assignment was to go to the Neuropsychiatric hospital in Kware, a local government in Sokoto, to preach and I had only one member. I tried every strategy I knew to grow a church; I was practicing it, yet it never worked. I said to myself, 'let me start baking cakes.' I would get someone to help me bake cake every Sunday while I carry the cake, visit them and give them the cake yet, they will eat the cake and not come to church. I was using my own wisdom to power a church–it never worked. Anytime I was asked how service was, I would reply 'great', even when the only church member had no offering to pay. He would even be looking up to me to give him transportation fare back home because he was a cleaner. This happened for months but it didn't affect my happiness, I still kept on going to Kware three times a week–Wednesday, Friday and Sunday with my motorcycle.

If death had an opportunity to get hold of me, I should have died because I loved overtaking cars with my motorcycle even while there was no helmet in Sokoto at that time. One vital lesson here is that anybody that is sending you on an errand is responsible for your feeding and protection. Serve the Lord, he will protect you. The day I thought I had a breakthrough was when there was fuel crisis in town; people who waited for cabs but couldn't get any reluctantly came for the service; they were being religious especially because they couldn't go back home. From one member, I saw ten. You could imagine how happy I was seeing the numbers rise from ten, twenty, thirty to fifty; I preached and prayed for them all. After the service, a man came to meet me asking 'Is this how you preach every Sunday?', 'yes' I replied. He noted that he could have been attending our service if he was pre–informed. The next Sunday, they all returned to their churches. Later, they started coming in tens, twenties until seventy five percent (75%) of those in Kware was in attendance. On one of the days, I noticed people were not comfortable, they weren't responding the way they used to respond. I didn't not know that the Chief Medical Director (CMD) of Neuropsychiatric hospital Kware had entered and sat down holding his Bible.

I had visited the CMD more than thrice, he would just look at me as I talked without any response even while I prayed. Sometimes later, as I was going to his place, the holy ghost instructed me not to go with my Bible. I was a bit confused because I knew I was on a mission to preach. He said, 'when you get to his place, talk to him about politics. Remember you are a graduate of political science'. As soon as I arrived at his place, the moment he saw me with no bible, he was happy. I sat down and talked about politics with him for more than an hour. The man that never said anything before was now going to escort me after the lengthy discussion. Guess what? The following week, he was in church. Thank God I read political science–*all things walketh together for good*; the knowledge of the course I read helped in convincing him. I and the CMD now became friends as he started attending our fellowship meetings. Stay where God has asked you to stay!

Jesus recognized that a lot of concerns arise for people as they serve God, so Jesus needed to trash it out. It started as a thought–Jesus looking upon them said, *'with men it is impossible, but with God all things are possible'* (Mark10:27). Peter began to say to Jesus *'…Lo, we have left all, and have followed thee.' (Mark 10:28)* There are people who feel they are putting in so much effort and it is not amounting to anything, people say 'we have served God but it doesn't seem to pay'. However, remember Peter must have been thinking to say 'we have left everything, look at our life. What is there to show that we are following you? 'Jesus answered and said *'…Verily I say unto you, There is no man that hath left house, or brethren, or sisters, or father, or mother, or wife, or children, or lands, for my sake, and the gospel's, But he shall receive an hundredfold now in this time, houses, and brethren, and sisters, and mothers, and children, and lands, with persecutions; and in the world to come eternal life.' (Mark 10:29–30)*

There are two things here–some are doing what they do only for 'his' sake but have not channeled it to the 'gospel's' sake and vice versa. Jesus said it must be the two, you need to find out whether you are doing the two: for his sake and for the gospel's sake. '...*he shall receive an hundred fold now in this world*'–not in heaven alone. I need to tell you that an hundred fold is not ten percent, it's far more than that.

What else shall he receive? He shall receive houses, brethren, he won't lack companion he can't be alone, there will be people to stand for him, he shall receive sisters, he shall receive mothers. You can see he left one mother now he shall receive mothers, he shall receive children'–not just his biological children but also spiritual children. He shall receive lands, persecution, troubles from those who hate him for the cause of the gospel in the world to come–eternal life.

Jesus told Peter here to relax; 'don't say you are serving me in vain, your service has its own reward'.

> *'And now, Israel, what doth the LORD thy God require of thee, but to fear the LORD thy God, to walk in all his ways, and to love him, and to serve the LORD thy God with all thy heart and with all thy soul, To keep the commandments of the LORD, and his statutes, which I command thee this day for thy good?' (Deuteronomy 10:12–13)*

HOW SHOULD WE SERVE HIM?

1.   Serving one another

'As every man hath received the gift, [even so] minister the same one to another, as good stewards of the manifold grace of God.' (1 Pet. 4:10)

You can't use what God has not given you. For whatsoever He has given you, use it as a gift to minister as a good steward of the manifold grace of God. If you are an engineer, use that platform to serve him, if you are a tailor use such to serve God. Let it not just be about you or the money you are making. Some of the people I have so much loved their sacrifices in our church are the medical people who are always ready to serve not just the people in the church but even Muslims. They have a heart for the people and they are willing to serve because they recognize that is what God has given them. What has he given you and how are you using it for the kingdom? He said we should serve one another as good stewards, faithfully helping one another.

2.   Not slothful but fervent in spirit

Not slothful in business; fervent in spirit; serving the Lord' (Romans 12:11)

I love it when I see young people that are choristers singing with passion and fervency. If yours is to serve God in such capacity, don't wait to be reminded. Every time you have to be reminded of your kingdom duty; you have lost it. You have to be *fervent in the spirit, serving the Lord.* Imagine a pepper soup that was prepared five hours ago but is now cold, would you love to eat it like that? While some people prefer cold food, the fact remains that it is sweeter when is hot or warm. Ensure your service is fervent! Sometimes I have to carry tables and chairs because I don't want to be told that such arrangements caused delay for a service.

The question is 'How did I get all these things God gave me? How will I get more?' God will surely give me. Did I ever know that I will see laptops or computers in my life? Now that I have them and they are in my custody to serve God for this generation, why should I be begged or persuaded to offer such in service to God?

3.   Serving God with reverence

> *'If any man serve me, let him follow me; and*
> *where I am, there shall also my servant be: if*
> *any man serve me, him will [my] Father honour.'*
> *(John 12:26)*

There is a way you go about life that compels God to bless you. There is also a way you about life that stops you from attracting God's blessings. As you serve him, the father honours you. Serve him with everything you have, I can't tell you that I have given my best to God but for the little He has blessed me with, I am giving it to God including my intellectual giftings.

The willing mindset

The first time I attended a webinar meeting via zoom, I saw the way it was being done. I said to myself, 'we can do the same thing in the church' since I have the kingdom mindset. I was once asked to make a presentation in an international school which I did well, after I repeated the same process the second time upon request, the school gave me a voluntary appointment in Huawei. I was rendering my service and then, an opportunity came my way. Today, we have had countless zoom meetings and webinar presentations. If all you care for is money, you will make the money but you won't make good money. Life is more than money!

Let everything God gives you be for the kingdom, for the advancement of the kingdom so that the father can honour you. Stop looking at others, do your part well. When money becomes your priority, you won't go far.

Never monetize your gift

We once called upon a music minister for a Pentecostal Fellowship of Nigeria (PFN) meeting, he directed us to speak with his manager. Upon calling the manager, we were asked to send a sum of five hundred thousand naira (#500,000). I immediately challenged him, 'for what? If you sing, will Lazarus come back to life? What are you singing? Why don't you see your coming to Sokoto as a means to advance the gospel? Indicate it on your curriculum vitae that you went to the Seat of the caliphate, a Muslim dominated area to sing and worship God? Why is money your priority? 'We called on another who told us he was booked but would only be available for a day. 'One evening is not enough. You may not worry, we have our own music ministers who will sing', I replied. That was exactly what we did.

Don't monetize your gift. The moment money start leading you, you won't go far. There are many people that were reigning, and before you know it, they are out. If we are paying music ministers to sing, how much then do we pay Ebenezer Obey, Sunny Ade–those who sing and carry their whole equipment to functions. Please, it is important that you use your gift to advance the kingdom. 1 Samuel 12:24 says we should be faithful in what has been committed into our hands. In that service you are rendering, be faithful while serving with all your heart. Money will naturally follow; people appreciate good things. Somebody may not pay you anything for five years, then in your sixth year somebody may appear and pay you for a labour of ten years. The kingdom runs based on mysteries. Serve God with all your heart, be faithful in serving him. Be ever willing to serve.

4.   Remain Stedfast

*'Therefore, my beloved brethren, be ye stedfast,
unmoveable, always abounding in the work of
the Lord, forasmuch as ye know that your labour
is not in vain in the Lord.' (1 Corinthians 15:58)*

Has somebody visited your house, shop or office and talked

down the church and the pastors? Have you stopped going to church because of such? You have to be steadfast, unmovable. Friends, Jesus gave you life, he gave you salvation. How much did you pay for all these? You have to serve God; he gave you peace of mind. I will rather have peace of mind than untold riches with no peace of mind.

Just because someone spoke to you in an unruly manner is not enough reason to quit your service in the house of God. Always know that your service is unto the Lord and not men. If you are in Christ, how come you are easily moved, always persuaded to go about kingdom service? That is not good enough. I have heard many things in my life that would have made me leave ministry including from family members. Due to the fact that I understand kingdom service, my conviction is rooted in what I believe. Don't let people's actions and inactions easily push you off kingdom service. The word of God says we should be unmovable, steadfast. It is not about men. Remember, it is unto the Lord not unto men. Hallelujah!

5. Serve without strive or vainglory

*'let nothing be done through strife or vainglory;
but in lowliness of mind each esteem other better
than themselves'. (Philippians 2:3)*

God wants us to serve him without anything being done through strife or vainglory. (Phil 2:1–11) I don't have anything against talent hunt but when it becomes competition; there are languages that are not permitted in the kingdom—'the best keyboardist, the best drummer, the best singer' is not allowed in the kingdom in as much as it is allowed outside the kingdom. In the kingdom, there are nothing as 'best' rather, we are meant to complement each other, Paul says 'what is it that I have received that is not given unto me from God?' If we have to do talent hunt to discover talents of people without necessarily involving picking the best, then there is no issue with it.

Identifying someone as the richest man *in the world* is allowed. Notice it is *in the world*; if anyone introduces himself/herself as the richest person in the kingdom, there is a problem. It means his/her money has not been used to serve the kingdom. By the time your money serves the kingdom, you can't remain the richest. Do you know how the bible describes Job?–the richest man in the east, not in the kingdom. There is nothing as 'richest' in the church. Today, we identify the most beautiful in church–young girls are now being paraded on the altar as beauty pageants. This also is wrong. We are all servants; it is the masters who determine the best. Scriptures say that 'that which is highly esteemed among men is an abomination to God', let us watch it.

We are not in a competition, we can never be in a competition, we are not competing with one another. What God asked me to preach is not what he told you to preach. What God has asked you to do is different from mine, just do it well. All manners of rivalry and hatred must stop among people. Romans 12:9–13

If you think you are the best, God always has a replacement.

He told Elijah, '*...I have seven thousand (7000) people that have not bowed to Baal*'. One day, a pastor came to our former church, on that day I happened to preach. When I finished preaching, he was surprised to see that somebody in Sokoto could preach such wonderful message. He opened and emptied all the money in his pockets, placing it on my hands as a seed. However, to come out and now arrive at a conclusion that I am the best because of that compliment would be a bias. Let nothing be done through strife, let nothing be done to show that we are better than other people. That can make God leave you *–Ichabod, the glory has departed.*

Have you read about what happened to Samson? He was still feeling anointed, he said to himself, 'I will rise up like other times,' little did he know that the Lord had departed from him.

63　　Offer service as a goodwill to the Lord

'With good will doing service, as to the Lord, and not to men:' (Philippians 2:3)

Render your service unto God with a goodwill and as you do so, remember it is *as unto the Lord.* One woman once told an usher in the church to stop shouting at her children stating that the reason why the usher did that was because she was not married. This left the usher crying. When the report got to me, I asked her, 'why are you crying? Is it unto men or unto God? He that repays evil for evil, evil shall not depart out of his house. When somebody is doing evil to you and you repay it with love, the bible says you are like somebody heaping a coal of fire on the other person's head. Render all your service in God's house as unto the Lord.

GRACE FOR SOUND OF ABUNDANCE

*'And Elijah said unto Ahab, Get thee up, eat
and drink; for there is a sound of abundance of
rain.'– 1 Kings 18:41*

WHAT DO YOU DO WITH a sound? You speak, vocalize, shout, say it out, forgetting whoever may be mocking. The best time to shout the sound of abundance is especially when everything seems to look difficult. In 1 Kings 18:41, 'Elijah said unto Ahab, get thee up, eat and drink; for there is a sound of abundance of rain'. In verse 43 of the same chapter, Elijah instructed his servant to go and observe the cloud for the sign of rain. The servant returned and said, 'I found nothing' but Elijah told him to keep checking until the seventh time when the servant returned saying, 'behold, there ariseth a little cloud like a man's hand' Elijah responded, 'arise, go unto Ahab, tell him to prepare his chariot'.

Knowing that we live in a wicked world where files are being hidden and people are set up, it requires that you need to speak out. You speak in the office so that your promotion can come. As a preacher, sometimes people laugh at me for what I say but since these words produce results, I keep saying them. I am not afraid to talk, I say that which I have to say, I back it up with prayers just like Elijah and then combine it with what Jesus said 'to sit down and work'–everything is workable if you sit and work. What then are the things you are to keep saying for the abundance of rain to come?

'For thus saith the Lord God of Israel, the barrel of meal shall not waste, neither shall the cruise of oil fail, until the day that the Lord sendeth rain upon the earth'1king 17:1

In the above verse are some of the things you should be saying; 'for thus saith the Lord God of Israel' inside your kitchen, inside your store, when you enter your kitchen 'in this season, the barrel of meal shall not waste, neither shall the cruise of oil fail until the day that the Lord send help to my house.' Every morning, you wake up and speak God's word! Sometimes when you are bothered about your survival, just put these words in your mouth and keep saying it; don't just think it. 'An opportunity will open, a job will come, a business link will come, opportunities open unto me.' When there's a sound of abundance, you have to make the right sound.

You can just be in your house and somebody comes knocking with a message, 'you know I just thought of bringing a bag of rice and a gallon of oil and three chickens for you. Your name keeps ringing in my heart; you may give it out if you don't need it.' Do you know that there are people in the church that you think that they have abundance but they don't even have what to eat, yet they are just grateful to God. They have learnt not to wear their problems on their faces; don't put your problem(s) on your head–there is a sound you need to speak. Sometimes ago, because of the way we had to cook for many persons in my house, being a pastor's house, a time came that my wife told me that the last bowl of rice finished. I told her that it couldn't finish and that another one was coming. Two days after that time, somebody came and gave us a bag of rice, saying that he was just in his house when he was inspired to give the token. In fact, he was a stranger. I wondered, 'so God heard me!' People keep quiet too much, choose to speak God's word!

THE TALKING FORCE

You have to talk, the world we live in operates by force, it doesn't operate on its own. There are people who have and will never give you until you beg, so you have to speak and make a sound so that a force will propel them to help you, else you may die in hunger. There is a sound of abundance of rain but somebody must make the sound, the sound here doesn't refer to abrupt noise, rather it is the word of God that must be sounded. You declare God's word to everything and then supply comes; this principle has not failed till date.

> *'Now unto him that is able to do exceedingly,*
> *abundantly above all you can ask or think*
> *according to the power that worketh in us'*
> *(Ephesians 3:20)*

This is part of what you need to sound, you have to say this out irrespective of whatever you are going through. 'Supply is guaranteed in the name of Jesus'–make this sound in every season.

There is need to put your hope in God–*And God is able to make all grace abound towards you that you always having sufficiency in all things may abound to every good work'* (2 Cor. 9:8). Keep making the sound of the word; the scripture is above anyone and everyone. Scriptures say that the word of God that comes out of His mouth will not return void, it is like the rain the cometh down from heaven to water the earth. Have you ever seen a scenario where the rain that wets the ground returns and decides not to give seed to the sower and bread to the eater? It's impossible–that is the word of God! You've got to wake up every morning and sound the word knowing that the word of God is spirit.

When you decide not to make a sound, nothing happens. *'Seek ye out of the book of the law no one of this shall fail nor shall lack her mate for my mouth has commanded it as the mouth is commanding, what happens his spirit will gather them.'* (Isaiah 34:16). As you sound the word, there is a gathering. If you don't sound it in the season of difficulty, the season might swallow you up.

*'But my God shall supply all your needs according
to his riches in glory by Christ Jesus. Phil 4:19.*

Around the period of coronavirus pandemic, somebody working with an airline said his salary was slashed into half. Later, they were told to go on a temporary leave since the airline was not currently in operation. I spoke to a young lady who said she was coming from north–eastern Nigeria and that she received a letter stating that bank activities had been reduced, hence they should proceed on a temporary leave. In spite of all these happenings in the country, you must understand that your case has a point of interception. You must believe that in the days of hardship and famine, there is divine intervention that takes place such that when people are sacked, your name is not included, rather, it attracts favour and more open doors come through for you.

*'According as his divine power has given unto
us all things that pertains to life and Godliness
through the knowledge of him that has called us
to glory and virtue…' (2 Pet. 1:3)*

We are not called to shame; we are called to glory, strength and virtue according to his divine power not my power but according to his power.

In Psalms 81 :10, God introducing himself says, *'I am the Lord thy God which brought thee out of the land of bondage. Open thy mouth wide and I will fill it'*. Proverbs 10:22 also says that *'the blessing of the Lord maketh rich and added no sorrow'*. Don't be quiet, speak! Decree that you are blessed. As you keep saying it, doors are opening.

Deut. 8:18 says *'you shall remember the Lord your God for it is he that giveth thee power to make wealth, that he may establish the covenant which he swore unto thy fathers as it is this day.'* You go ahead and say 'Lord, I receive power to get wealth'. As you keep sounding this, the Lord keeps moving and positioning you, arranging and organizing everything in obedience to Christ. If you think because you are serving God you will experience shame, that's a lie!

When a man is blessed, ideas comes, you are full of ideas and when you are full of ideas, resources will not be a problem. If there is anything I have enjoyed by the grace of God, it is ideas that I have been blessed with. I am not just after the spiritual wellbeing of people but I am also concerned about their total development; what a man sows, he will reap. Sometimes, you talk today and you keep quiet tomorrow, sometimes you are too discouraged to talk, you are not persistent, Jesus tells a story of a persistent widow who would not allow the judge to rest, the judge said to her 'I don't fear God at all, my problem is this widow—she comes every day and wearies me.' The bible records that the widow got what she wanted.

Some people might even want to mock you, but you have to keep saying it, 'My God shall supply all my needs' I have been saying it for long, now my children have joined me in saying it because they can see the result now. The way I declare it aggressively now was the same way I said it when I was still riding a motorcycle. A man looked at me one day as I repaired the plug of my motorcycle, saying 'my God shall supply my needs', shaking his head, he went his way. I met that man sometimes back on a motorcycle and I now ride a car. Who has God supplied his needs? He had a car then that made him look like a local champion, that was why he despised me. Keep sounding the word even when it doesn't look like it, sound it when there is nothing on ground. Ideas will come, opportunities will come, they will surely come!

Deut. 28:6 says *'blessed shall thou be when you come in, blessed shall though be when you go out.'* Decree that you are blessed in your going out and coming in in the name of Jesus; sound it–it is a sound of abundance. Hallelujah!

3

THE INNER STRENGTH

'… You've gone through a process in your life full of crisis and you are back, yet you are still okay. You can smile, laugh and you can still do more than you were doing before. When we see that, we call that 'inner strength"

GOING DOWN MEMORY LANE, I remember a friend some years back who got born again and was rusticated and didn't know he had been dismissed. The case had been brought before the academic committee of the university where the decision was taken. He was writing his last paper when a lecturer walked in, saw him and recognized him. 'Stand up I know you! What are you doing here?', he said. In response, my friend said that he was writing his last paper and the lecturer said 'No! Two years ago, you were rusticated, you were asked to leave. I was a member of the panel and that decision is still standing.' He took his paper, tore it, and asked him to walk out of the class. That's inner strength!

Strength is meant for you to be able to carry out a task. For some people, suicide becomes the next option in a case like my friend's. Imagine that he would have thought of what he would have to say to his expectant parents. When we, the brethren, heard it, we gathered but didn't know how to comfort him. That's why the bible talks about the comfort of the Holy Ghost. So, we went there and sat down like the friends of Job waiting for the right time to talk and we waited, guess who broke the silence? Him! He told us not to worry, that he was born again and had nothing to lose. 'I will just find another school and start all over again', he said. How easy would that be, having to start all over again? He replied, 'for I know that all things work together for good…' (Rom. 8:28) 'I am now a child of God,' he continued 'if God is in Heaven and he saw this and didn't stop it, I know something better is ahead'. That was such a display of inner strength that moved me, today, he is a Ph.D. holder.

You can look very strong outside yet be very weak inside. Have you seen people that look very strong outside but they are very weak inside? Your physical strength is not so useful particularly when you are not in a 'jungle' kind of society where you need to fight physically to survive. If we are to be in the jungle, the muscles would have relevance for survival. There and then, the physical strength is everything. Peradventure your job is related to that which requires you to lift something daily, then your physical strength is so important. Inner strength, just as the name implies, cannot be seen. Why is it called inner strength?

It is so called because it is an off–shoot of what comes from within, hence it can't be seen.

How do you access my inner strength? Would you say I am strong because I'm smiling? How then do you measure a man's inner strength? You can determine such in times of crisis, in trouble and some other things you will see shortly. Crisis has led some people into smoking, drinking, pornography and all manner of crimes. They are alive but their lives have been mutilated and squeezed; something terrible has happened to their lives. This is not what inner strength connotes. It simply means that you've gone through a process in your life full of crisis and you are back, yet you are still okay. You can smile, laugh and you can still do more than you were doing before. When we see that, we call that 'inner strength'.

I remember the case of a lady who was going to get married, it was two weeks to her wedding, she got home and discovered that the man she was going to get married to was already married with two children. Wedding cards were all out, some people had travelled with her and then they discovered that the man had two children and the wife is still alive. They had placed the cards all over the working place. The wedding was cancelled yet she still came back and continued her work, it was quite painful. When I saw her, I didn't know what to say to her I was a bit careful but she was the one smiling and saying 'pastor how are you?' Later, she got married to another person. What do you call that? Inner strength!

Your ability to recover from a fall shows whether there is

strength in you or not. Everybody experience crises but it just that the crises are different. Some go through marital crisis, financial crisis, emotional crisis, academic crisis. When you develop inner strength, it helps you to accomplish many things in your life. You will face situations in life, people behaving in a manner you don't expect, betrayal. You are going to see relationship that is meant to lift, bringing others down. Prayer won't stop all of these things. So, get ready for some trouble on your way to destiny.

WHYDOWENEEDTODEVELOPINNERSTRENGTH?

1.   **Accomplishment of great tasks:** You need inner strength for some tasks, I call them 'great tasks'. When you are asked to undertake such assignment, you may become scared. If you don't develop strength, you will run away. Even before the assignment begins, you may find yourself saying 'I am not called for things like this'. You begin to develop a lot of languages. In Joshua 1:7, God tells Joshua, "only be thou strong and very courageous' In verse 9, He repeats the same.

When the strength on the inside is not enough, you may end up procrastinating, you tell yourself 'I will do it next year, next month' You can't accomplish any great task in your life if you have not developed inner strength.

You can't take cities, territories, you can't develop anything special if you don't develop inner strength.

Dispelling discouragement: You will meet with discouraging situations in life on the path of destiny. You will meet with some situations that you didn't plan for. *'And he said unto me, my Grace is sufficient…'* (2 Corinthians 12:9–10)

We were praying at a time in 2019, little did we know that a situation like coronavirus pandemic was ahead. We didn't plan for it, yet the season consumed many people, organizations, and Jobs. The season has changed the way we live, it has produced new slangs amongst others. If you don't develop inner strength, you will faint or die. Hence, inner strength is necessary because there will be discouraging situations.

The game may change, not giving you what you bargained for and you begin to say 'but this isn't part of the plan, this is not part of what I have written down', Yet, now that it has come, you have to face it and keep moving. Lack of inner strength can lead a man to looking for an alternative that is not good. Yet, God says 'my grace is sufficient for you. *Therefore, I take pleasure in infirmities, persecution and distresses, in reproaches in necessities for when I am weak, when you think I am dying, I am getting stronger! I am looking beyond the challenges, hopelessness, loss, set back.*

Yesterday is gone, you have only today, enjoy every day of your life. When you find yourself in the unpleasant situations of life, find a means to enjoy it. Don't let your world start changing, don't let your world collapse. Just know that God is in charge, He says "my grace is sufficient for you, my strength is made perfect in this weakness", then, you see God's strength.

Remember that light shines brightest in the midst of darkness.

2.   **Maintaining Vision:** Another reason why you need to sustain inner strength is when you need to stick to the vision God has given you in life, you need that strength. Has God called you to do certain things and it seems like plans are changing, things are not going the way it should go? There is every likelihood you change the assignment to suit you, yet God says 'No, I'm sending you there for a purpose.' You need to maintain strength to keep the vision going when things are not going in the direction you want.

> *'Watch ye, stand fast in the faith, quit you like men, be strong'– 1 Cor. 16:13*

The real man is the man who stands by what God wants him to do in spite of the changing circumstances. This is the same thing for marriage, a real man is the man that stands by his word even when things are not going the way it should go. Your love for your wife hasn't changed, your love for God hasn't changed. You are still willing to carry on. You have to stand and be strong, else you will find yourself changing assignment and vision every day. Be consistent, maintain a tempo, you will soon break forth, your testimony is on its way.

I used to know of a woman who, when her husband lost his job, was making up for the man's role. Everything was still looking normal, only those of us close to the couple knew the man had lost his job. The woman kept helping and guess what? That season didn't last for two days, it lasted for years yet the woman was consistent. You need to stick to the original vision God gave you in the midst of changing situation. After this time, the man got a job better than the one he had lost eight years ago and the first car he bought, he gave it to his wife. Some women might have left saying that they don't want to suffer.

Sometimes, things don't go well for people God has called for an assignment. There are seasons of life that things may go the other way round. While I was coming up as a young pastor, it wasn't very easy for me. Some of my friends I told that I was going to be a pastor were not only laughing, they were pitying me. They were already predicting what would befall me in ten years' time. The kind of suffering that awaited me, one of them said, will be more than what Paul went through. Really, the way life was at that time gave evidence to their claim. There was nothing tangibly evident for me in ministry, there was in fact no salary. When eventually I got something to use as official car, it was a vesper that was sent to me from Nnewi.

I was pastoring the church in Kware then, I started with one member. I had to go there three times a week. In fact, a friend said he was praying one day and he saw that three trees collapsed on myself and Apostle Martins Atanda. I said 'God, these are the people that should encourage me!' In fact, some group of church members told me to go and get a job because the bible says that the idle man should not eat. They told me that what I was doing was idleness and that I should work. I was warned that if I continued in that manner, Hunger will kill me. You need to maintain your vision even when things seem discouraging, the bible says 'who has despised the days of little beginning?'

It was in that condition I met my wife. My brother was living with me because I was more like the most successful person, at least I had a vesper. Five of us were living in one room, so when I met my wife, I took her there. As a corp member then, her salary was four times more than mine. Several people approached her, saying 'you came all the way from Port Harcourt to serve here, and you want to marry this person that is thin like a broom' Even some of my friends discouraged her. I cannot over–emphasize the fact that you need to stick to the vision. God had told me I was going to be a pastor. While I was serving in 1995, God told me I was going to be a pastor all my life so I knew that, I prepared for it. If God has given you a vision, stick to it. You can do this only by developing an inner strength

3.   Taking the 'first step assignment': Inner strength will help you take what I call "The first step assignment" The inner strength produces boldness in you. Don't be afraid to take the first step assignment, you may fail. All you have to do is to retrace your steps and start again. When you need to take the first step, deal with your fears. If you don't build inner strength, you can't take the first step for business, relationship, schooling and so on – I call it 'the first step mystery.' There is always a first step for everything in life; some people have taken the first step and they are still taking steps, while some have refused to take the first step and they do not take any until twenty years later. What's that first step you have to take? Rise and do it today! It could be business wise, marital wise or otherwise.

A writer I follow, the late Myles Munroe said the richest place in the world is not the gold mine, nor the mineral mine, he describes the richest place in the world as the burial ground. According to him, at the burial ground, there are books that were never written, houses that were never built, relationships that never started and several people that have died with hidden potentials because they refused to take that one step. You can start from somewhere; do you know a book of five hundred pages started with page one? As a matter of fact, you will become very suspicious if you see a book of five hundred pages with no first page. How about if page one has a content that summarizes the entire book. So many people have refused to do anything great in their life because there is this spirit of fear that is always telling them 'if you start, it will not work'. There is this spirit of unnecessary comparison that has engulfed many people. You keep seeing the person that started something and it never worked.

> *"For God hath not given us the spirit of fear; but of power, and of love, and of a sound mind."***1 Timothy 1:7**

God hasn't given us the spirit of fear so where did you get it from? Some people will not do anything in their lives because of fear. Many have died out of fear, some people are carrying sicknesses in their body, the one they created because of the fear of such sickness. Many times, people have read somethings that have caused them to bear fear. Scriptures say that you have a sound mind, not a deformed mind. Go and start that business; if you are persuaded about getting a loan, go and get it. Write down how you intend to repay it. I am of the opinion that you don't spend 30% of whatever you borrow, you keep it so that you can start repaying with that. Stop dreaming about releasing an album, bring it to the physical. Start somewhere, you will be shocked that the world is waiting for you but you have refused to unlock.

> *'So do not fear, for I am with you; do not be dismayed, for I am your God. I will strengthen you and help you; I will uphold you with my righteous right hand. ... So do not fear, for I am with you; do not be dismayed, for I am your God.'– Isaiah 41:10*

God says you shouldn't fear; deal with your fears. God has ordained you to be an employer of labour yet you are still being paid salary because you have refused to take a bold step. You have to disengage the spirit of procrastination. Do you know that for that thing you have set your heart to do, God has put the money, resources for it in the hands of someone? You have not accessed it because you have refused to talk about it and take that bold step. Some people's destinies are tied to what God has told you but the problem is with you; you have refused to start. You keep thinking, 'If I start now, this thing might not work'. Why don't you just attempt to start it first?

Somebody approached me in my office sometimes ago asking me to pray for her business, she was into the sales of handmade bags and shoes, I was so happy with that. I asked if the bag and shoe she had on her were made by her too. Her response was in the negative, 'No', she said. 'Why should you not be wearing the shoes and bags you sell?' I retorted. That's unwise! If you are making people buy things that are not good with prayers, then you are 'a witch'– that word means 'to manipulate people'.

Don't forget this, take the first step. Why? You can't continue to have yourself held under fear.

A reservoir for the waiters: Assuming that after you must have worked and achieved some level of success, suddenly you begin to drown. How do you cope? The inner strength becomes like your reservoir, from where you draw sustenance.

> *'But they that wait on the Lord shall renew*
> *their strength; they shall mount up with wings*
> *as eagles; they shall run, and not be weary; they*
> *shall walk, and not faint.' (Isaiah 40:31)*

Are you beginning to have some set back even in the midst of that achievement? Wait upon the Lord and renew your strength.

> *'Be of good courage and he shall strengthen your*
> *heart, all ye that hope in the lord'– Psalms 31:24*

> *'And God is able to make all grace abound towards*
> *you that you always having all sufficiency in*
> *all things may abound unto every good work'*
> *– 2 Cor. 9:8*

God wants your 'work' to be good–develop that strength. There is a lot to do in our generation even in the midst of situations that are challenging our world. You should be asking God what the best thing to do is; don't put your life on default. Seek God's face on the changes that you need to undergo, yet, the inner strength within you must be developed so that you don't get so discouraged and then you aren't willing to move again.

One of the ways to develop inner strength is to renew your communication with God in the place of prayer plus a ceaseless time of worship before Him. You tell God 'I am not going to be discouraged'. Stick to what God has told you, if he has told you that he will lead you on what to do, he will surely make a way where there is no way. Always know that for every task you have been given, you need inner strength.

Say this prayer:

> *'Lord, I am taking this first step; let your strength*
> *be made available for me in Jesus in Amen.*

4

THE HOLY GHOST

'And the Lord God formed man of the dust of the ground, and breathed into his nostrils the breath of life, and man became a living soul' (Gen 2:7)

THE BREATH OF GOD CAN make you become something you will never have imagined. The Pentecost is not just for speaking in tongues, it is to take our world for Jesus. The holy ghost is not a joke, this is why the younger generation is losing interest, they think the holy ghost is all about speaking in tongues.

'In the beginning God created the heaven and the earth. And the earth was without form and void; and darkness was upon the face of the deep. And the Spirit of God moved upon the face of the waters' (Gen. 1:1–2)

For a long time, the bible has been talking about the Spirit of God, representing it with water, wind, fire. In Gen. 1:1–2 above, God was not moved because of the absence of light, shape, or life because He already had a solution and that solution was 'the Spirit of God. 'The Spirit of God moved upon the face of the earth, and God said, 'let there be light' and there was light–that settles it. We change our world by the breath of God.

Today, we have more people in church that are not born again, they are in church departments yet they are not born again because they have not encountered the holy ghost. Being born again is beyond the four walls of the church, it is about power, power for everything. With the holy ghost, God created the heavens and the earth, He set the world in his beauty, the lord made the earth without pillars, he made the boundaries for the water that they should not crossover.

You can come afresh in the holy ghost and turn your world upside down. We must not narrow the holy ghost to that which is done in the church. Our families must feel the presence of the holy ghost. We are supposed to take the holy ghost into our businesses, academics, private lives, and let the light of God shine in us. Paul says 'I am not ashamed of the gospel of Christ for it is the power of God unto salvation'. The gospel doesn't reduce anything; you don't have anything to contribute to the gospel but the gospel has everything to contribute to your life. We need to embrace the ministry of the holy ghost; people listen to songs that don't edify and come to church to lead worship; this is why there's no encounter. He is called the holy spirit, so when you add an unholy thing, he can't work.

> *'And it shall come to pass afterward, that I will*
> *pour out my spirit upon all flesh; and your sons*
> *and your daughters shall prophesy, your old men*
> *shall dream dreams, your young men shall see*
> *visions:' – Joel 2:28*

Remove the holy ghost from my life and life is zero. It is only when the holy ghost is absent that you can slap your wife. The bible says 'grieve not the spirit' You can partner with the holy ghost in managing your business, men will wonder what your secret is and you tell them 'it is the holy ghost, the Spirit of the living God 'That is the realm we are moving into.

People who brought this move of the spirit just reduced it to miracle and speaking in tongues in church, this is not supposed to be. We must relate the holy ghost to our world, we have to go above what men are thinking, bringing the holy ghost to everything. My friend who is a medical doctor was in the theater room sometimes ago where he was operating, during an operation something went wrong, a vein was touched and blood was gushing. The professors around were confused about what to do because the patient was losing so much blood, so from inside the theatre room, he put a call through to me, I prayed with him and he received an idea on what to do and that was it, the blood stopped! They said to him, 'this is not in the field of medical science'

You can't be a Christian only inside the church, the holy ghost should help you make the difference. There are realms of glory, there are dimensions in the spirit. We must move to the spirit dimension on a higher level, we can't remain in the same level forever. What are you receiving on the day of Pentecost power? God is giving you the power to make wealth. (Det. 8:18) The holy ghost makes the difference. *I will pour out my spirit upon all flesh…'–* (Joel 2:28) You have to decide to be a part of the recipient of the spirit. You are a carrier of God's spirit not just for speaking in tongues; speaking in tongues is a sign, signs are meant for changes. In Ezekiel 37, the prophet was taken to the valley of dry bones, God asked him 'son of man, can these bones live? 'He answered 'Sir, I don't know', 'speak to the bones, you bones, hear the word of the lord!' and the bible says that flesh came upon the bones, but the bones did not move. Again, God told him to prophesy to the wind.'…*prophesy, son of man, and say to the wind, Thus saith the Lord God; Come from the four winds, O breath, and breathe upon these slain, that they may live.'*, he said *'breathe upon this flesh that they may live, so I prophesied as I was commanded and the live and breathe came upon them, an exceedingly great army.* 'The breath of God is what we celebrate on the Pentecost.

You are alive to demonstrate the power and the glory of God. (Isaiah 11:1–3) You must understand that you are not an ordinary man, most of the young people feast on satanic things, that's why they are limited. The spirit of creativity is leaving us, we just have pocket out of millions rising, there is an adage that says that 'a rich man in the midst of many poor people is poor'. Until we bring back the holy spirit, the spirit of creation, only then can he rest on young people. We have spoken in tongues for so long and nothing has changed in our lives, the holy ghost shall make you of quick understanding such that you understand what is happening and what to do. The unbeliever shouldn't be better than you because you are a carrier of the holy spirit. My desire for this generation is a change, the poor people we have in church now are too many, the number of people looking for food to eat are up to 70%; food, clothing and shelter are called the basic necessities of life, it is the lowest part of life and that is where many are currently, most people that are working are engaged in such for food, clothing and shelter. The holy ghost is meant to make us the light.

'And when the day of Pentecost was fully come, they were all with one accord in one place' (Act 2:1)The Pentecost had not fully come in genesis, Ezekiel and Joel, it came in Acts 2.If the Pentecost had not come then, yet we saw those dimensions, now that the Pentecost has come, we should see more. In Acts 2:1–4, they all spoke in tongues as they were given utterances, you don't have to remain in one level, move to another dimension. You should be able to interpret tongues, the holy ghost must affect all aspects of our lives, Paul said *I am not ashamed of the gospel*, this is the time to demonstrate the holy ghost.

Desist from seeking joy from mundane things, it is only the holy ghost that gives joy. Go for the holy ghost. There is nothing that gives joy and full satisfaction like the holy ghost. I challenge you to make room for the holy ghost. You can't put yourself in the world and in God at the same time, you have to choose one. We must have something to show that we have the holy ghost. You must have something to show as an adamant follower of the holy ghost. May the holy ghost bring you to a level of influence, connection, impact and wealth.

5

UNCOMMON FAVOUR

"I will lift up mine eyes unto the hills, from whence cometh my help. My help cometh from the Lord, which made heaven and earth."
(Psalms 121:1–2)

EARLIER THIS YEAR, JANUARY TO be precise, I said that the season ahead will be very challenging. Meanwhile, there was no spread of coronavirus yet. I had to address some of our pastors, friends and church members urging them to get ready due to the upcoming challenging season. Some ministers said the year will be very rosy while very few said the years will be challenging as we have it now. Very surprising is the unpreparedness that surrounds the season. It is not just the coronavirus that is the problem but the implications that came with it. I read sometimes ago that a particular company laid off fifty thousand workers because it couldn't continue to pay workers' salaries. For a country like Africa that depends on other countries like USA, UK and China for help, we have now come to terms that those lending their hands of help to us are also affected. Most young people didn't feel so much pain because they were able to get allowances from their parents, some companies are on the verge of closing down, some nations like Nigeria that have built their economy on petroleum and some other sectors have come to terms with the fact that the amount of a barrel has drastically dropped.

Global organizations and other organizations are still standing but in a continent like Africa, the palliative effort to give something small to reduce their plight in some places is ridiculous. A lot of money has been pumped out in a country like Nigeria for instance but the pact of corruption would not let such funds get to the poor masses. All these are indicators to reasons why it is not an option in this season, but a must, to connect to God. It is a must and we can only trust God. I was discussing today with someone sometimes ago, I didn't know the week was to be Easter Sunday simply because it didn't look like any celebration was on its way especially with the presence of lockdown without food, light and water in some places.

WHAT IS GOD SAYING?

It is important to understand how to survive in a country like ours and if there is any message from God to us this season, it is the message of **uncommon favour**. The season is very complicated–people are asked to sit down at home, people are getting depressed because our society is not a sitting society rather our society is a hustling society, full of strugglers more reason why you don't tell people to stay at home without doing anything. The situation is very terrible in our nation but somehow in the midst of the terrible situation, God has a record of separating some people while he cares for them, making them look as if they are not part of the problem.

In John 5:1–13, we see how Jesus went for just one man in the midst of all the people because of exceptional favour. Somehow in our prayers, God has a way he answers but the same God will tell us if there is a situation that will occur; we are beginning to see them. Psalms 91:1–16 notes, *'He that dwelleth in the secret place of most high shall abide under the shadow of the Almighty, I will say of the Lord he is my refuge and my fortress my God.in him I will trust. Surely, he shall deliver thee from the snare of the fowler and from the noisome pestilence, he shall cover thee with his feathers'*

Notice that the prayer was made for an individual, this is because certain people are always exempted from trouble.

> *'He shall cover thee with his feathers and under his wings shalt thou trust; his truth shall be thy shield and buckler. thou shalt not be afraid for the by night; nor for the arrow that flieth by day; nor for the pestilence that walketh in darkness; nor for the arrow that flieth by day; nor for the pestilence that walketh in darkness nor for the destruction that wasteth at noonday. A thousand*

*shall fall at the side, and ten thousand at the right
hand but it shall not come near thee'*

May God make a demarcation for you in Jesus name!

*'you will only see with your eyes, you will only
hear with your ears but it shall not come near
you, because thou has made the Lord, which is
my refuge even the most High, thy habitation,
there shall no evil befall you (evil of hunger,
lack and stagnation), neither shall any plague
(such as coronavirus come near thy dwelling).
For he shall give his angels charge over thee to
keep thee in all thy ways. They shall bear thee up
in their hands lest thou dash thy foot against a
stone, thou shalt tread upon the lion and adder
the young lion and the dragon shalt thou trample
under feet. Because he hath set his love upon
me, therefore will I deliver him; I will set him
on high because he hath known my name. He
shall call upon me, and I will answer him, I will
be with him in trouble; I will deliver him, and
honour him. with long life will I satisfy him and
shew him my salvation.'*

This is the word of God, receive it! The bible says we are to
receive the engrafted word with meekness. God has created
a rest for the people of God but some don't receive it because
of unbelief. Some people hear the word of God but it doesn't
mix with faith in their heart so it didn't profit them.

Decree these words: 'I receive the word of God into my life and it profits me. No plague, no disease will come near my dwelling in the name of Jesus.

Allow those words to mix with faith so it can be performed in your life. Psalms 91:14 says '*...because he has known my name*', Let your love be on God, it pays to seek God.

In Luke chapter 4, Jesus told his disciples how that even in his hometown they couldn't receive the word of God. Receive the word of God, it will help you. In Jesus' narrative of Luke 4:25–26, the bible didn't say that *there was a widow*, it says *there were many widows* but Elias was just sent to one. There was a woman that enjoyed uncommon grace, favour and attention. Widows were dying, we even read of cases where women had to eat their children because of the famine at that time. This was during the days of Elijah when there was no rain in Israel. A particular woman cried out, saying *'O King! there is trouble here'*. The king said, *'how can I be of help to you? Is it from the barns? Just tell me what the problem is'*. She replied, *'I and this woman had an agreement that we were going to eat our children, so we boiled my child and now the other woman is hiding her own.'* What a horrible situation!

Jesus, trying to make a hard statement said,

> *'In the days of Elijah, I tell you the truth, there were many widows. When the heavens shut up three and half years when there was famine… Elijah was not sent to anyone except this widow.'*

*'And many lepers were in Israel in the time of
Elias the prophet; and none of them was cleansed,
save Naaman the Syrian'–Luke 4:27*

The Lord restored the flesh of Naaman to that of a child. This is how to get prepared for the season, any season at all–receive the word of God and confess it every day. It doesn't matter what you see or hear, confess the word every day!

I need to remind you of the need to possess the spirit of faith, knowing how faith works. Position yourself in a place where faith is built and not on what destroys faith. What you see and what you hear every season determines the direction of your life. Therefore, your word should be charged with faith. Although we are law–abiding people, we should wear faith as a garment. You should run away from anything that can shipwreck your faith, any reckless lifestyle, any iniquity lifestyle that will thwart your growth. Paul said some people have **made a shipwreck of their faith.** Speak faith, keep faith and see faith. Keep it from pollution and iniquity so that when you speak, heaven will hear you when you need to address a matter and respond to you.

All the places you hope to get help from may be going through the worst phase of their lives. Countries like America and major cities in Nigeria today are looking for help per time. ***I will lift up my eyes unto the hills from whence cometh my help, my help cometh from the Lord.*** 'Let your gaze be on God and not any human being, else you would miss the help of God.

Conclusively, let your gaze be on God. Yes! He sends human beings to help you but let your attention not be on the messenger but on the sender. As you continually see God in your imaginations and your prayers, supply and favour will come your way. This is not the season to run away from God. Deuteronomy 8:18 says *'you shall remember the Lord thy God for he gives you power to make wealth'*. If you don't value prayers, you don't expect to be on the same page in life with those who pray. I tell people, 'if you come to ask me for help, all I can render is crumbs compared to what God will give you', so make yourself available this season.

Say to yourself: 'I receive Gods word this season; I receive favour this season in the name of Jesus.'

6

VICTORY IN CHRIST JESUS

'The victorious life in Christ Jesus cannot be possible without a connector'

WHEN JESUS RESURRECTED, THERE WERE three major things that he did, there were other things he did too. I am going to be emphasizing the three things that characterize his resurrection. Of all graves, only Jesus' is empty, it's a proof that he is alive, a proof that he conquered death, and that he has given you and I victory. Let's consider these three emphases from Luke 24.

1. **The struggle of Jesus:** He struggled to make them understand that his resurrection is a fulfilment of scriptures.

2. **Validation of the scriptures:** After his resurrection, the first thing he did was to make them understand

the validity of scriptures, he went further to break bread with them as a symbol of his resurrection and the futuristic symbol of the unity of the body of Christ

3.   **The blessing:** The third thing he did was to bless them after which he took his leave. He didn't depart without a blessing for them.

Beginning from the struggle after his resurrection, we see that this is also a struggle for us today. Understanding the validity of scriptures, believing it and paying attention to it remains a challenge for the believer today. Jesus was talking to them so much about the scriptures yet they seemed not to understand. At a point in Luke 24:25, Jesus said *'oh fools, slow of heart to believe what the prophets has spoken, ought not Christ to have suffered these things and to enter into glory and beginning at Moses and all the prophet?'*

Beginning from Moses who wrote the book of genesis, Jesus began to explain scriptures to them about the things that were written concerning him that they were now experiencing, yet finding it difficult to believe. It is not just about shouting 'resurrection', do you believe in the resurrection? Do you believe in the power of the resurrection? Do you believe in the scriptures that talk about the resurrection? Those scriptures have come to pass. What this means is that all that God has said about your life in the scriptures will come to pass. As he explained, they were still doubting, saying 'we went to his tomb but we couldn't find his body'. In turn, Jesus condemned them of unbelief.

What is your response to what God has said of you in the scriptures even when you have not handled these promises? Your response should be to live according as he has said. Jesus had to start with Moses because Moses had said that a time will come when the brazen serpent which was risen would be hung on a tree and whosoever looked upon it would be made whole. *'The seed of the woman will bruise the head of the serpent'* (Gen. 3:15), Jesus was explaining all these to them, yet they were not getting it. From genesis to the prophets, he got to Isaiah 53 and he was hoping they would understand, he proceeded into psalms, *'…lift up your head, O ye gates and be ye lifted up ye everlasting doors, so that they king of glory will come in. Who is this king of glory? The lord of hosts, He is the king of glory'* (Psalms 24:7–10), *'The Lord is my shepherd, I shall not want'* (Psalms 23:1), he reminded them that he was that great shepherd yet they still didn't understand. Meanwhile Jesus was to be caught up into heaven and these were the same people that would continue the work.

It was at the table of the communion that they eventually got all that Jesus was saying to them, that's why the place of the communion in the church is essential. The communion was the second thing he did, at once their eyes were opened there. May your eyes be open to see the things that have been said concerning you in Christ Jesus. That is where our hope and assurance lie only if we believe. 'Didn't our heart burn within while he talked with us on the road, and while He opened the scriptures to us?' (v.32) The communion is a fulfilment of what Jesus has said through his prophet in psalm 133, *'how good and pleasant is for brethren to dwell together in unity, it is like the precious oil that flows down the skirt of is garment because he said there lord has commanded his blessing* 'There is no blessing in hatred, there is no blessing in division but there is blessing in love and unity. Everytime there is breaking of bread, there is a manifestation of Jesus.

Jesus stood in the midst of them and said 'peace unto you' and they were terrified and afraid and supposed that they have seen a spirit and he said unto them 'why are you troubled? why do thoughts arise in your heart? look at my hands and my legs' and why they yet believed, he asked, 'do you have any meat?' 'There is power in communion. This is where our cruise as Christians lie, in understanding the scriptures not just its reading. This is the delivery of God's revelation in your heart that provokes an activation for destiny.

THE BRIDGE BETWEEN YOU AND VICTORY

Why was Jesus so concerned about understanding the scriptures? It is because that is the only thing that is missing in our days, our understanding of the scriptures is poor. When Jesus rose, he took his time to explain the scriptures because they needed to understand the scripture above what anyone is saying. You must give attention to the scriptures. There is no blessing without an understanding of the scriptures. To be blessed is to be empowered because you will encounter challenges in life that will want to make you doubt the existence of God and what He has told you. The reason why many are not enjoying the blessings of God is not because blessings have not been pronounced on them, it is because there is no connector–many Christians have nothing to connect to the power that God has released. This explains why you can have light over your house and live in darkness, you can have water in front of your house but when you refuse to connect, you might be carrying buckets around, seeking to fetch water.

The victorious life in Christ Jesus cannot be possible without a connector, it is your humility and readiness to learn and connect that gives you a guarantee of access. You might have been prayed for yet you are still in defeat, depression, sin and untold hardship. Before ascending into heaven, Jesus blessed his followers and empowered them even before the holy ghost came, he called them blessed, that they cannot lack, that if they are sick, they will be healed–that is what it means to be empowered. To leave above all the things that push other people down, there needs to be a connector. Here are two important connectors:

1. **The spirit of understanding**: Nations are poor not because they don't have the resources, but because they lack the understanding of how to process the resources at their disposal. You can have resources and not use it because you lack the understanding. It will interest you to know that Jesus spent time gaining understanding, we are people of great knowledge but no understanding. Paul would always pray for understanding, the spirit of wisdom and the spirit of knowledge for the church because he knows those things are key for life. The reason why we are not enjoying many things is because

we lack the understanding of how to access it, we may have the information but may not know what to do with the information. Knowing that 'by His stripes, I am healed' is an information until you process it with the second connector. Else you will still die of sickness; you have to process what you have heard.

2.   **Faith**: The second connector that processes what is inside understanding is called 'faith', the ability to believe. Collating scriptures is like getting grains (that is knowledge), you then have to determine what you want to make the grain into (this is where understanding comes in). At the level of being a grain, it is information. We all have grains but as we begin to process it in our spirit, it produces results for the purpose we desire. If you lack the understanding, you will not be able to maximize the information you have at your disposal to get the multi–faceted results that is available–this is faith. A lot of people have information, some even know it can be used to achieve different purposes but they have never processed it themselves. That is why the bible says, ***'faith is the substance of things hoped for, the evidence of things not seen'***

When faith begins to process what is inside understanding, it leads to confession. The things you hear and see make your life change because ***'faith cometh by hearing and hearing the word of God'***. If your life is not changing, check what you are hearing.

We have two missionaries in our local assembly, Sunny and Elisha, they couldn't even write letters but they now interpret for white people from America. Why? This is because of what they have seen and heard. How can you not be changed with what you hear and see? Much more reason why Jesus told his disciples to be careful of *'what you hear'*–there are some things you close your ear to. As you enter into the scripture, you are entering into another kingdom. You need to learn the art of the kingdom, the language of the kingdom, the conduct of the kingdom and the victory of this kingdom.

In conclusion, resurrection is not just jamboree, it is a time of restoration and blessing but you must have a connector. Remember the bible says 'I can do all things through Christ who strengthens me'

I declare you blessed, step into the victory that has been occasioned for you by the reason of Jesus' resurrection in Jesus' name.

THE WONDERS OF GOD

WHAT WE CALL THE WONDERS of God is an experience that is possible only to them that understand the 'holies of holies.' It is a realm where you can know everything by the spirit depending on where you are standing. You can be in church and not be in the holies of holies, rather, you are at the outer court. You can preach, sing very beautifully from the outer court. The holies of holies used to be a physical place in the old testament but it is now a spirit realm. This realm requires consecration and purity of heart. It is in this realm that you know the heart of God for every season, knowing what to do. When famine was coming upon the whole earth, God told Joseph what to do. God has always spoken in the scriptures about what to do. Don't trade the wonders of God, the wonders of his presence for anything.

What we do in the 'holies of holies 'is to worship God, to worship Him in spirit and in truth (John 4:24) This does not necessarily refer to singing, rather, it describes a life style. Worship means adoration, to place as relevant. Your time can become worship when you make it relevant to God, including your life–all about you. When you come to that realm, you must know what is happening, it is a realm where Satan has no power over man. The holies of holies the place where worship is done.

'1I was given a reed like a measuring rod and was told, "Go and measure the temple of God and the altar, with its worshipers. 2 But exclude the outer court; do not measure it, because it has been given to the Gentiles. They will trample on the holy city for 42 months. 3 And I will appoint my two witnesses, and they will prophesy for 1,260 days, clothed in sackcloth." 4 They are "the two olive trees" and the two lampstands, and "they stand before the Lord of the earth."[a] 5 If anyone tries to harm them, fire comes from their mouths and devours their enemies. This is how anyone who wants to harm them must die. 6 They have power to shut up the heavens so that it will not rain during the time they are prophesying; and they have power to turn the waters into blood and to strike the earth with every kind of plague as often as they want.

7 Now when they have finished their testimony, the beast that comes up from the Abyss will attack them, and overpower and kill them. 8 Their bodies will lie in the public square of the great city—which is figuratively called Sodom and Egypt—where also their Lord was crucified. 9 For three and a half days some from every people, tribe, language and nation will gaze on their bodies and refuse them burial. 10 The inhabitants of the earth will gloat over them and will celebrate by sending each other gifts, because these two prophets had tormented those who live on the earth.

11 But after the three and a half days the breath[b] of life from God entered them, and they stood on their feet, and terror struck those who saw them. 12 Then they heard a loud voice from heaven saying to them, "Come up here." And they went up to heaven in a cloud, while their enemies looked on.

13 At that very hour there was a severe earthquake and a tenth of the city collapsed. Seven thousand people were killed in the earthquake, and the survivors were terrified and gave glory to the God of heaven.

14 The second woe has passed; the third woe is coming soon.

The Seventh Trumpet

15 The seventh angel sounded his trumpet, and there were loud voices in heaven, which said: "The kingdom of the world has become the kingdom of our Lord and of his Messiah, and he will reign for ever and ever."

16 And the twenty–four elders, who were seated on their thrones before God, fell on their faces and worshiped God, 17 saying: "We give thanks to you, Lord God Almighty, the One who is and who was, because you have taken your great power and have begun to reign. 18 The nations were angry, and your wrath has come. The time has come for judging the dead, and for rewarding your servants the prophets and your people who revere your name, both great and small—and for destroying those who destroy the earth."

19 Then God's temple in heaven was opened, and within his temple was seen the ark of his covenant. And there came flashes of lightning, rumblings, peals of thunder, an earthquake and a severe hailstorm.' (Revelation 11)

The altar of God is the place of prayer, a place where you bend your knees.

The scriptures speak about measuring the place of prayer, measuring the place of sacrifice, measuring the people that are also worshipping therein. Who exactly is a worshipper? Go and measure it and come and tell us! In other words, measure those who came with their spirit, because there are many who come with their bodies while their spirits are absent.

People go to church for different reasons. Some people go to church and they feel comfortable talking from beginning to the end, so many things bring people to church. Hence God says 'go and measure them, measure all these people. To survive any season, your heart must be with God, not in a crafty way, it must be fully with God. Where you are standing when you come into the holies of holies from where you worship God is very important. When you remain at the outer court, the name of God is mentioned, at the outer court there are emblems that look like God but those people at the outer court do not have God at the center of their worship. At the outer court, you might just attempt to project self. This is why that physical location is no longer as important as the spiritual location.

For a worshipper of God, the only thing that is at the centre of your pursuit is God and nothing else. You don't need to encourage them to do anything for God, they are eager to do it. It matters whom you are standing before whether in church, at home or anywhere at every season. There is no season when you should play religion or be a part–time Christian; there is no time that you should live outside the court and pretend that you are in the holies of holies. You must understand that where you go, things you say are all important. He told the angels not to measure the outer court because it is not part of what matters. If you are a worshipper, you worship him in

Spirit and in truth.

Most times, we forget that we are standing before the almighty God, the Bible describes Him as 'the God of all the earth'. God must become your desire in the place of prayer, worship and singing, in everything. When your life counts so much, even if death wants to lay hold on you, heaven will say 'no' because you have been marked, so you can't be touched. ***'These have power to shut heaven, that it may rain not in the day of their prophecy, they have power to smite the earth with all plague.'*** (verses 6–14). The big question is 'are you ready to come into the holies of holies to have an unusual relationship with God and also become conscious of God in your life and around you? 'To be conscious of the God of the whole earth in whatever you do is to be aware that you are standing before the God of the whole earth, the one that can kill and make alive. You can't live with the conscious of God and still want to live your casual life, living a careless life.

THE CHALLENGE OF OUR DAYS

In times past, for a country like Nigeria, the focus of our prayers has been on Boko haram, afterwards we can now see the difference between the scores of people that have been killed in ten years by this sect compared to the ones coronavirus has killed per week, globally. Indeed, something worse has come upon the face of the earth. Choose not to live the way you have been living before, you can't wake up and just decide not have communion with God. This is the season to rearrange your life and destiny, to reconsider seeking God again, there may come another season that is worse than this coronavirus era, irrespective of the time you are reading this book. There can be a season worse than these seasons we are talking about–prepare, readjust your life, there is no stubborn man before God–that only exists in the realm of men. Before God, everything bows, the hills skip, the mountains melt, the sea roars, the sea saw God and started going back, death and destruction saw him and fled.

During the coronavirus pandemic era, I read a story about thirteen billionaires who travelled to a distant location to purchase a particular island where there will not be coronavirus and as such, they can enjoy themselves but they were arrested. They were instructed not to come down from their plane. Then I asked myself, where are all the casino? Do you not understand what is happening this season? The stadiums are empty, the studios are empty too, yet you are still not taking your life serious with God. Car factories are empty, planes are grounded, jets are grounded. In fact, the President of the United States of America is incapacitated; before the coronavirus pandemic emergency, nations were displaying their arsenals but during the pandemic, they were all grounded. The nuclear deal they refused to sign is not even necessary again, the lord of the whole earth is walking through the earth and angels are in heaven singing,

Who is like unto, oh Lord?

Who is like unto thee oh Lord?

Among the Gods, who is like thee

Glorious in holiness and fearful in praises

Always doing in wonders. Hallelujah

The almighty is walking through the earth he created quietly, and the whole inhabitants of the earth are asking for His help. Men have been forced to bow to the Lordship of Jesus, men have been forced to call upon God, the whole world is looking unto Yahweh, it seems like we exceeded our boundaries. Who shall not fear thee oh God! Leaders are helpless, yet the almighty is lord!

My prayer for you is that you come into the total consciousness of God and forever behold His wonder.

8

GRACE TO PUSH THROUGH

'Weeping may tarry for the night but joy comes in the morning.' (Psalms 30:5b)

DID YOU START WELL BUT you have given up along the line because you met with opposition, demonic interference or otherwise? God has spoken to you to keep pushing, don't give up! In Genesis 26, there was famine in the land where Isaac was. God appeared to Isaac and said 'stay and work here, I will bless you.' You should not allow situations to dictate what happens to you, rather let the word of God dictate to you so you don't end up like Abimelech and other people in the Bible. Abimelech, upon hearing that there is bread, took all his family there and in the course of searching for a better life, he lost his life and his two sons. Hence, it is important that you know what God is saying per time on what business to do, what work to do, what instruction to follow. Then you keep pushing, it will get better. In God, everything changes, it is when you are out of God that nothing works.

When grace finishes in a marriage, a break up is bound to take place. There will be ten, hundred and a thousand reasons to break up. When grace finishes in a man's life, everything begins to pack up. He begins to say things like 'oh! I don't like this Job again, now I'm relocating to Port Harcourt' When God sends you to Port Harcourt, he backs you up, but relocating to Port Harcourt because you want to get a better job there may not mean that things will work out there. Let God be the one leading you to move. When grace is upon a man's life, the desert can turn into rivers, when grace is available, we say 'God will make a way where there is no way'. It is therefore important that God's grace is evident upon our lives that we may not lose confidence in God.

In Hebrews 10:35, we are admonished not to cast away our confidence, if you can hold unto it, it has a great recompense of reward. The issue is that you don't know how many years your waiting period will be, so you need to ask God. If you don't ask God, people will push you out of your waiting stage. Some years ago, a relative became very apprehensive and concerned about me, wanting me to come to America. I had declined her request, I said 'No! this is what God is calling me to do. 'She told me that I could pastor in America but I consistently refused because God has not called me there. You need to stay consistent on it before God can trust you to bless you with resources. Where God has sent each of us is different, as for me, God has sent me to Sokoto, not another place. There was a time Apostle Martins Atanda told me God had instructed him that the work in Abuja should begin and he asked me, 'do you want to go?' After I prayed about it, there was no leading for me to go. 'I can't force you to go, I was the one God told about going to Abuja, I am leaving', apostle replied. As at then, the church which I now pastor wasn't full–fledged as this, yet he entrusted things into my hands, knowing that things will get better and this I assured him about. I have been a full–time minister since 1997, performed differently while I became full time overseer over the church ten years ago. You don't give up easily, keep pushing. If God calls you to do something, don't leave it.

The fact that something is not working is not a reason to give up on it. When something has been commissioned into your hands, you wait long enough for it to work. In my years of discharging pastoral duty, I am not sure I counted a million naira that was mine till I was forty years old. As a Masters student, I was that poor till I was forty years old but it was not enough reason to run away. As a masters holder, my official 'car' was my bike and luckily for me, I found a wife that fell in love with me even while I cruised my bike. With the bike, we visited our members from house to house. I refused to give up, even when people challenged me to find something else doing. *'weeping may tarry for the night but joy comes in the morning.'–(Psalms 30:5b)*

The problem many a times is that people are in a haste; they have people around them who tell them many things in a bid to put them in haste, they can't wait! Meanwhile before you wait, ask God, 'is this where I should wait?' If God tells you not to wait, then you've got to move to another place. Let your relocation be by God's instruction, not by instinct, not by what you feel. Scriptures say, 'eyes have not seen, ears have not heard neither has it entered into the hearts of men, what God has planned for those who love him.' Be a lover of God, not silver nor gold, not car nor a big congregation. Just be a lover of God! He will test the love. Even while all manners of advice came my way, I told people that the person that called me was God and not man. Meanwhile as at this time, there was nothing; I was looking like somebody that needed sympathy! Never give up!

While we were at Kotokonshi, there was nothing, we were sitting in a church surrounded by grasses, we had members containing about sixty five percent (65%) students. Who would have even given offerings? People would walk up to me after service to tell me that there was no food for them to eat, yet God said 'stay! keep pushing, if I tell you stay, stay!' The same thing applies to marriage and every other thing in life. Just stay when He says to stay, let people laugh and talk, let people see visions. It is a choice that people challenged; the only person that never challenged my choice was my wife. If many people share their stories today, you will be surprised. You must understand that there is nothing that you are going through that somebody hasn't been through. You need to hear other people's story; some people's stories are worse than yours. Some people have gone through the four walls of death, yet they survived it. I saw the four walls of poverty but I didn't give up. One of the things I learnt in my years is not to beg or meet people for help, even when I couldn't afford to feed well.

There are some offers that if I had taken, they would have blocked the doors to my tomorrow. When I was given such, I rejected it. What are you going through that will make you compromise as a young lady? Is it because you need a job or because your family is suffering and you want to help them? How far can you take care of your family by exchanging your body for a job or for money? How far can you pull your family with such? No! You resist such job! As you denounce such and exit, they might remind you that your suffering continues, you say 'yes Sir!' There's a way to turn God to intervene on your behalf and there's a way to turn him off. When you start acting as if you can do it all by yourself, then God leaves you alone but if you wait on God, if you put your all on God, men can't stop you. As you keep forging ahead with what He has told you, men can't stop you.

What are you going through that has changed your lifestyle? You have stopped your prayers, no bible study in the name of seeking for job or business. That is Satanic, not a blessing! Anything that takes away your bible study, your prayers and attendance of church meetings is no longer a blessing but a curse! It's a trap of Satan. Whatever God has not given you is bound to kill you. There are things you don't accept because they will block future opportunities–it will kill your tomorrow. They will kill that big thing that God is keeping for you.

You don't have to see any man as your end, else, heavens will never open for you. Sometimes, we pray that God should open the heavens for other people so that they can be a blessing to us, we don't pray such for ourselves. Ninety–five percent

(95%) of people that will give you anything will do so only from their crumbs, only five percent (5%) will give you from their treasure. The bible records that those who went to see Jesus gave from their treasure. Do you know what it means to bring from your treasury? When you give from your treasury, you will feel it. A treasury house is not a place where you keep little currencies. Before you get anybody that will give you from his treasury, they are just five percent (5%), this is because people have plans. So, you must ask God to open your heavens without being desperate in your request.

There are people you see today who are rich, but in five years' time, you won't find what they call riches with them again because it is all gone. The bible makes us understand that riches have wings; it can fly away and if that's where you put all your hopes, you end up being frustrated. Why should you change your name, your religion, your identity because of a job? If there is something better, you will never touch it if you can't wait on God! You want God to give you a miracle that is not cut with human hands, then you have to wait! You've got to wait on him!

Today, I am being consulted to get people for jobs even at international level, there are things you don't want to do so that it doesn't block the bigger one; you know why? You have no idea of what tomorrow will bring. Yesterday, Chief Olusegun Obasanjo was in prison, tomorrow, he is on the throne. Do you know what tomorrow holds? If you are too bothered about now, you will suffer for it in the future. Esau would agree to just anything, that was how he lost it to Jacob. This is why the bible says *'And I hated Esau and laid his mountains and his heritage waste for the dragons of the wilderness'–(Malachi 1:3)*. Spiritual things didn't matter to Esau.

There is a grace to push through and push well. Revelation 22:13 reads *'I am alpha and omega, the beginning and the end, the first and the last.'* 'Whatever He starts, he will not abandon, he will finish it. He doesn't leave his projects half–way, why should He start in the first place? Philippians 1:6 says that *'God who has started this good work in you he will finish it.'* When agitation gets too much, it makes someone take wrong decisions, cut corners.

BE STILL AND KNOW THAT I AM GOD

This was God's word through Moses to the children of Israel at the heat of indecision before the Red Sea. You need not try to take shortcuts; God has something better for you. Only God lifts men, not your boss nor any man. However, when you put your trust in a man, you can't go beyond the level of such man. A man cannot raise you beyond his hand. If I have to carry someone now, I can't raise such person beyond my hand, If I am to do otherwise, it means something else is carrying him, if I still have to carry him, he has to be between my hands.

Be careful how you attach yourself to human beings in the name of partners and helpers, they can't raise you beyond who they are. When you reduce yourself to a collector and not a giver, that's how you will be treated. May God not catch your eyes fixed on somebody.

> *'Thus saith the Lord; Cursed be the man that trusteth in man, and maketh flesh his arm, and whose heart departeth from the Lord.'–Jeremiah 17:5*

The bible says in the passage above that cursed is the man that puts his trust in men, when good is coming, such man shall not see it. You are not allowed to put your trust in man, not even your relatives. Not even in my relative would I place my trust; else my life would never have been balanced today. If God sends you, he will make a way, you don't need to lie. When you can sit down, tap into God's resources and invade your life with his goodness, men will invite you worldwide.

> *'Brethren, I count not myself to have apprehended: but this one thing I do, forgetting those things which are behind, and reaching forth unto those things which are before'–Phil 3:13*

I forget the things that are behind and I keep pressing forward, am not allowing the things in the past even though they may seem good, they may be bad, nevertheless I'm pressing forward. 'The good' sometimes has refused to allow some people go, 'the bad' can also pull people back. Whether it is good, bad or ugly, I'm pressing, am pressing towards the mark for the price of the high calling of God in Christ Jesus. In 2 Tim. 4:7, Paul says 'I have fought the good fight, I have finished my course, I have kept the faith' (testimony intact). The testimony is important. Nobody has said you won't get the money you need. Only if you will wait where God has asked you to stay. Some claim to be waiting, but they are not where God has asked them to stay.

Paul says to Archippus 'take heed, be careful that you fulfill the ministry. 'Be careful that you fulfill your destiny. You will see many strange temptations, know God. Even when I had the opportunity to enter the villa, I didn't eat, I saw people excited to eat inside Aso rock villa. God instructed me not to eat anything. I was sent for three times, yet I declined. I was told that His Excellency said 'even if it's a cup of tea', I told them 'the most high said, no water'.

Be careful of how you live, be careful of the things people call 'favor' and 'partnership' There were people who ate in the bible and that was their last. Maybe if I had taken that tea, I will have exchanged a greater portion for something less. Some people don't know what they have exchanged in their lives. There's a grace to finish well. See Zachariah4:9 and Nehemiah 6:15; *'The hands of Zerubbabel have laid the foundation of this house but I tell you, his hands shall finish it and thou shall know that the lord has sent me unto you.'* May your hands be strengthened to finish strong in the name of Jesus Christ. At last, the wall was built in Nehemiah 6:15, that was the same wall that brought shame and reproach, it was completed in fifty two (52) days.

PRAYER

Pray to receive strength and peace from the lord so that you don't bow to pressure. You may be taking a decision that might injure you. God, I receive your inner peace, for whatever decision I take, let it be by you. Amen

GRACE FOR TOTAL SHIFT

'For a shift to happen, there must be an exchange of power. Without the involvement of power, it will be a mere talk.'

As I PRAYED ON ONE of the mornings, God laid it strongly upon my heart that many people were due for a new season. I could sense a new season, like Elijah, I could hear the sound of abundance of rain and what I kept saying and I am still saying is the prayer that the rain will come.

'For the kingdom of God is not in word, but in power'–1 Corinthians 4:20

For a shift to happen, there must be an exchange of power. Without the involvement of power, it will only be a mere talk. Scriptures say that the kingdom is not in words but in power; we have been talking about it but this is the time to enter into it. For that which you have been confessing, may God confirm them all in Jesus' name.

Psalms 62:11 says *'God hath spoken once; twice have I heard this; that power belongeth unto God.'* When power comes in contact with a superior power, gate opens on their own accord, opportunities surface, lost positions are retaken by people. He spoke once but twice have I heard, that power belongs to God. Psalm 63:2 says *'To see the power and thy glory in the sanctuary.'* This talks about the power of God being displayed that people may see and acknowledge God. There is a great need for people to get this realm, we need people to take over some things, business, politics amongst others. Those of the occult need to have a touch of the real power found in God.

I once prayed for some young boys who entered into trouble in Sokoto town, they were made multimillionaires with ill–gotten wealth, even though they looked so innocent, so simple. A corp member who had just finished service stole over fifty million of their money. They told the corp member to kindly return the money and that they had forgiven him; they were actively engaged in a legal business but from a wrong source. They were involved in forex trading and they were making terrible money from it, but the source was terrible, so things started to backfire. How did they come about such huge money? I asked. They buried life animals in town, the animals die while the number of maggots that came out from the decomposed bodies was the number of people that visited them for business. Now that things were backfiring, they needed the intervention of God because the same source of their money was now after their life, so they came for prayers. Eventually, they ended up in Sokoto prison and they lost everything. If you think Satan will prosper you, get the money and discover what comes after. This is the good news–there is the almighty that has power. 'Say unto God, how terrible art thou in thy works; through the greatness of your power, your enemies shall submit or bow themselves unto you.' There is power with God.

Shifting is possible because of power. For whatever has kept you down, may the power of God shift you in the name of Jesus. It is not about what you have, the Lord said to the children of Israel, 'go to Horeb and I will meet with you there'–Mount Horeb is a place of encounter. They enjoyed that encounter so much that they decided to stay there just for God to look for them in the next season of life and discover that they were no longer there. God said to the angels 'where are these guys?' the angels replied 'they are still enjoying Mount Horeb where you came down and spoke to them', He said to Moses, 'tell them that they don't have to dwell in that place for too long'. Is it about what you have achieved? Is it about where you ought to be that you are not? If God has destined you to be a billionaire and you are being worshipped as a millionaire, you are a failure! It is not about what you have but where you ought to be that you have not shifted to.

Declare this to yourself: 'I am shifting from one realm to another in the name of Jesus. I refuse to be stagnant; I am shifting. Devil, whether you like it or not, I am shifting, I am going to another realm, you can't keep me here forever.'

'He showed his people the power of his works, that he may give them the heritage of the heathen'–Psalm 111:6

GOD'S PROMISE TO YOU

God has promised you and I the heritage of the heathen, are you still in doubt about this? Reading your bible closely, you will discover that the day God transferred the heritage of Laban to Jacob, he gave him a blank cheque to choose first, in a short time, the wealth of Laban was transferred to Jacob. Laban's children were angry with Jacob because he had possessed all the wealth their father had. When power flows, anything is possible!

GOD'S MANDATE FOR OUR GENERATION

God is out to raise fearless prophets, men with boldness that will walk into a governor's office and say 'good afternoon Your excellency, you have been embezzling people's money, return it or in seven days' time the earth will receive you'. You turn back and he says 'let me go and drop you' and you tell him that you came with your own entourage, 'I am not poor'. What God is doing is not just to give you money alone but he is doing his work in our lives in all ramifications.

Consider Rev. 11:6, *'These have power to shut heaven, that it rain not in the days of their prophecy: and have power over waters to turn them to blood, and to smite the earth with all plagues, as often as they will.'* This is not just for pastors; it is for everyone who desires it. Governors, rulers will seek for you because of God's declaration from your mouth. When you send a text to a governor and you say 'in the next four days, there is a cheque somebody is bringing to your office, ensure you don't sign it because it is a fraudulent cheque' then after four days, somebody comes and gives the governor two beautiful cars, bringing out a cheque for the governor to sign. As soon as the governor remembers what you said, he says 'no, I am not signing this.' After a finding is conducted and it is discovered that it was true, you will be sought after. They will have to ask, where is that prophet? Nobody will ask you where is your church, you will only become the governor's prophet.

When you tell him 'sir, we are going for second term but you have to do what is right because righteousness exalts a nation, sin is a reproach to any people; when the righteous rule, the people rejoice but when a sinner rules, the people mourn.' They will be compelled to look for you. I have had access to sit with gubernatorial candidates before and I look at them in the eyes and tell them the truth, at least, you can't bribe my anointing. So God is anointing people–fearless prophets, prophets that will go to robbery scenes and say 'give me water', and then he says 'except those that came to rob in this bank will not use water, they will pick all their corpse seven days from now', you empty the water and you are gone. Everywhere will remain quiet because such has not happened before. When it happens, you will be sought after. These fearless prophets have the power to shut the heavens.

We need more dangerous prophecies that will make the enemy sit down, nobody has been able to terrify those in the place of authority. To terrify them, you don't need to go to presidential villa; you just pay for a press conference let them publish it in the best newspaper and you declare judgement upon unrighteousness. If they change, nothing will happen. By the time the effect comes, an emergency parliamentary session will be called to reverse ungodly policies while they will secretly look for the prophet. The bible says that when sentences against the wicked is not executed, more people will do the unrighteous. Indeed, there is genuine power with God.

> *'Ah Lord GOD! Behold, thou hast made the heaven and the earth by thy great power and stretched out arm, and there is nothing too hard for thee:'–Jer. 32:17*

EXAMPLES OF THOSE WHO SHIFTED IN THE BIBLE

- **Jabez:** He decided that things were not to going to continue in the hard way for him and then he prayed about it; he was shifted. (1 Chronicles 4:10)

- **Esther:** Esther did not only shift but her entire race also shifted. The Jews went on fasting and prayers (Esther 4:6) and there was a shift.

- **Jacob:** Jacob, at a point, was left alone and he wrestled with an angel (Gen. 32:24) He encountered a supernatural being and his life was changed, even his name was changed from 'Jacob' to 'Israel'.

- **Hannah:** In 1Samuel1:13, Hannah prayed her heart out and she experienced a shift. The bible records that what was taking place in her heart couldn't come out through her mouth but after that encounter, a shift happened. The one that was called 'barren' now had children (1Sam 2:21). The Lord visited Hannah and the result of the visitation was conception. She bore three sons and two daughters–there was a shift.

- **Israel:** God caused a shift for the children of Israel shifted (Deuteronomy 29:29). God brought them out with an outstretched arm, Pharaoh thought it was a joke, he drowned with his men in the sea, the sea ended his career.

- **Nehemiah:** In Nehemiah 1:11, Nehemiah was a cupbearer but he shifted from being a cup bearer to a governor in Nehemiah 5:14. He was appointed as the governor of Judah.

- **David:** The young man, David shifted from fighting against a lion and a bear in 1sam17:34, although they were great achievements. When God sent Samuel to anoint David, the palace opened for him. Which is better, to be a shepherd all your life, fighting against lion and bear or to fight and kill Goliath?

- **Joseph:** There were several shifts in the life of Joseph. Infact, Satan thought he had finished him, Joseph landed in prison for an unjust cause but in due time, he shifted to becoming more than a governor, he became one that the nations of the earth began to consult. His story was summarized in Psalms 105:19–22 thus; *'(19) Until the time that his word came: the word of the LORD tried him. (20) They king sent and loosed him; even the ruler of the people, and let him go free. (21) He made him lord of his house, and ruler of all his substance: (22) To bind up his princes at his pleasure; and to teach his senators wisdom'*

There has to be a shift for you, you are not going to remain on one spot in Jesus' name.

10

GRACE FOR THE SOUND OF VICTORY

'And one cried to another, and said, Holy, holy, holy, is the Lord of hosts: the whole earth is full of his glory. And the posts of the door moved at the voice of him that cried, and the house was filled with smoke'–Isaiah 6:3–4

THE DEVIL IS NOT AS powerful as you are thinking, it is where you place a man that you find him, you are the one that has placed Satan so high that's why you think he is powerful', I said as I spoke with a couple sometimes ago. You spend five days binding and casting Satan, yet you forget about the Holy ghost; is it only Satan that possesses people? Haven't you heard that the Holy ghost also possesses people? Why are we not talking about people being possessed by the Holy ghost? It is whatever you talk about that you will see, that's why we have painted Satan as seeming to be everywhere.

'And after these things I heard a great voice of much people; saying Alleluia; Salvation, and glory, and honour, and power, unto the Lord our God' Rev. 19:1 (KJV)

Take note of what the voice of the people in the passage above was saying, were they saying 'oh God! my car was stolen but I have Jesus, my children were kidnapped yet I have Jesus'? No! While those needs are good yet we see that multitude of people in heaven are saying 'thy will be done on earth as it is in heaven', they are saying in heaven; 'hallelujah, salvation, and glory and honour and power unto the Lord our God'–this is the sound of victory. As you wake in the morning and your feet touches the ground or even before that, you are saying 'hallelujah', you are sounding it! Why? You need to do so, it is not that you are meditating, you say it!

How more can heaven intervene on earth if we are not doing what is done in heaven? How can the heavenly beings intervene on earthly issues when we are so apart? When it is not in the manner of the way it is done in heaven, even our 'Hallelujah 'doesn't produce much power now because they have been made jokes. See how the heavenlies are saying their 'hallelujah' with a great voice.

What is this sound of victory?

The sound of victory is not the song you sing, it is the words that make up the song. As you sing 'I love you; I love you God', as we worship, you must recognize that only one person sits on the throne, that is why you don't worship Him sitting down; only one sits on throne. When you worship, only one person receives the worship–the one who sits on the throne.

> *'(2)For true and righteous are his judgements; for he hath judged the great whore, which did corrupt the earth with her fornication, and hath avenged the blood of his servants at her hand. (3) and again, they said; hallelujah and her smoke rose up for ever and ever. (4) And the four and twenty elders and the four beasts fell down and worshipped God that sat on the throne, saying, amen; hallelujah'–Rev 19:2–4*

Why the 'amen'? They are for all the needs you brought before God but 'hallelujah' must first go up. This is why you keep saying it–it is a sound of victory. You say it day and night in the car, in the plane, everywhere you find yourself. As you are saying it, the earth is taking record because they are sounds of victory.

> *'(5) And a voice came out of the throne, saying praise our God, all ye his servants, and ye that fear him both small and great. (6) And I heard as it were the voice of a great multitude, and as the voice of many waters, and as the voice of mighty thundering, saying, hallelujah; for the Lord God omnipotent reigneth.' (v. 5–6)*

This is what you keep saying as you make the sound of victory–

'Hallelujah, omnipotent, the all–powerful reigns!' Can you imagine that somebody is being taken to the theatre and as he is being wheeled, he says 'hallelujah, for the Lord God omnipotent reigns!'?One of these two things are bound to happen, either the doctors discover that the problem is gone after they open him up or he will not even go to theatre again. I have prayed for somebody that was being wheeled into the theatre because she had difficulties in given birth, they had bought everything that will be used for the operation. The person said, 'wait, let me call my pastor! 'Though I wasn't in town, over the phone I said 'in the name of Jesus.'As she said 'amen' to my prayers, she didn't have to enter the theatre. The doctors said that if there was nobody, the baby would have jumped on the ground, there was no need to push the baby out'–for the Lord God omnipotent reigns. There are songs you sing that angels branch to join in singing the song with you unto God.

> *(7) Let us be glad and rejoice, and give honour to him: for the marriage of the lamb is come, and his wife has made herself ready. (8) and to her was granted that she should be arrayed in fine linen, clean and white: for the fine linen is righteousness of saints. (9) and he saith unto me, write, blessed are they which are called unto the marriage supper of the lamb. And he saith unto me, these are the true sayings of God. (10) And I fell at his feet to worship him. And he saith unto me, see thou do it not: I am thy fellow servant, and of thy brethren that have the testimony of*

Jesus: worship God: for the testimony of Jesus is the spirit of prophecy. (11) And I saw heaven opened, and behold a white horse; and he that sat upon him was called Faithful and True, and in righteousness he doth judge and make war. (12) His eyes were as a flame of fire, and on his head were many crowns; and he had a name written, that no man knew, but himself. (13) and he was clothed with a vesture dipped in blood: and his name is called The Word of God.

Hallelujah! Salvation, and glory and honour be unto our Lord!–the sound of victory. Who will sound the victory over insurgents, kidnappers, sickness; who will? Who will sound the victory so that witches and wizard can flee? Let them know that God reigns. Who will sound the victory of our God everywhere? The Lord reigns all over Nigeria, all over the world!

'(3) And one cried to another, and said, Holy, holy, holy, is the Lord of hosts: the whole earth is full of his glory. (4) And the posts of the door moved at the voice of him that cried, and the house was filled with smoke'–Isaiah 6:3–4

The Lord reigns! While you are in your house, in the church or in the office and you are not sure of what is going to happen, you are not sure whether sickness or death is coming, you should sound 'holy is the Lord of host, heaven and earth is full of his glory.' As you keep sounding it, there is nothing that refers to you in what have said but the victory belongs to you–it is the sound of victory.

The latest statistics shows that eighty percent (80%) of Nigerians live in abject poverty, what is your future if you don't stay connected to the depth of God to bring out solutions? Yet, you still want to be a Christian and live like an unbeliever–then, you are a big loser. We have to make the sound of victory upon the wicked and corrupt Nigeria. If you ever get access to National assembly, you have to sound it; if you are a journalist, you have to sound it; even as a cleaner, you sound it–the Lord reigns. If you can't shout it out, say it gently, 'the Lord reigns', even if you are inside government house, say it–'the Lord reigns.' In Isaiah 6:3–4, *as they were shouting the post of the door moved, and the voice of him that crieth, and the house was filled with smoke*–What a strange encounter!

'The Lord is gracious and full of compassion, slow to anger and of great mercy. 'Psalm 145:8 Sound the graciousness of God, it may be that you are sounding it to deliver a nation; it maybe that an outbreak of flood is about to consume a community in California and as you sound 'the Lord is gracious, slow to anger and of great mercy', God puts an end to the flood.

> *'Say unto God, how terrible is thy works!*
> *Through the greatness of thy power shall thine*
> *enemies submit themselves unto thee.'–Psalm*
> *66:3*

What you do is to keep echoing it, they are sound of victory.

As I conclude, you can collate your scriptures for sound of victory, it must not be any scriptures about you but it must all be about God. He is a great king over all. Imagine you enter into the camp of killers and you don't know what to do against them, all you can do is to shout the sound of victory. When a problem comes, instead of shouting negative words, sound 'for the Lord most high is terrible and is a great king over all the earth. Hallelujah.'

> *'For the Lord most high is terrible; he is a great king over all the earth.'–Psalm 47:2*

> *'Great is the Lord, and greatly to be praised in the city of our God, in the mountain of his holiness. Beautiful for situation the joy of the whole earth, is mount Zion, on the sides of the north, the city of the great king.' Psalm 48:1–2*

Sound it aloud that the Lord reigns!

11

BUILDING CONFIDENCE FOR SUCCESS IN AN UNWILLING WORLD

'Cast not away therefore your confidence, which hath great recompence of reward'–Hebrews 10:35

THE WORLD MAY NOT BE willing to cooperate but God is determined to make you a success, He is committed to blessing you. The world is not willing, that is why we keep getting all sorts of news. Sometimes ago, a medical doctor who is a consultant was killed in his house in Gusau. What a world! What a waste! What is it that the man might have done that he can't be forgiven? Do you know how many lives that man would have saved if he was kept alive?

Hebrews 10:35 notes, *'Cast not away therefore your confidence,*

which hath great recompence of reward'–My greatest store of confidence is in God. There is no apology about it, you know that our greatest store (where we store confidence) is in God. Every other thing will fail, money will fail, career will fail, business will fail but on Christ the solid rock, we are building our confidence. In building your most holy faith, you keep building! If you lose your confidence, you can't do anything in life. If you throw away confidence, it is a problem, but your confidence should not be derived where it can't be sustained. Don't put confidence where it can't be sustained, don't put confidence where it cannot last. Placing confidence in your job is disastrous, what if you are fired? What if the man helping you is fired?

YOUR CASE IS DIFFERENT

A man told a young lady sometimes ago because he tried to molest the lady and the lady would not agree, 'Do whatever you can do, if I don't have you, you can't work in this organization. Go and ask about my records.' All the way, he forgot he was speaking to the wrong person. The young lady replied, 'Well, you can't have me, somebody else already has me', 'Who the Hell has you?', he retorted. 'Jesus!', she said. The response fell upon him as a great thud, he kept quiet because even if you are an unbeliever and someone gives that response, you wouldn't say 'Jesus should go to Hell!' The man condemned her, describing her as the 'church, church' kind of person. The young lady looked at the man and said 'my case will be different', 'let us see!', replied the manager, then she left. After some few days, this man was sent on an assignment and somebody else replaced him on the seat; while he was going through the files and saw the credentials of this lady, he gave her a call.

Immediately she entered the office, she recognized the man although the man couldn't recognize her. 'I have gone through your CV, the modern–day CV is about what you can do', he commented. He further quizzed her on why she was not offered the job in the first place. In turn, the lady narrated her ordeal with the previous man and how she refuted, claiming to have given her body to Jesus. She also spoke on the threats posed to her while she yet remained audacious. Perplexed, the man asked, 'is this true?' Yes! She responded. When the man returned, he was questioned on why the lady wasn't considered for the job. He tried to find excuses to evade his original intention. After the matter was let out to the shame of the man, oral interview was re–conducted for those that had been given the job as a way to let justice take its place. After the interview process, the young lady came out the best.

When you are a child of God, God will not only baptize you with the spirit of speaking in tongues and give you salvation, he will touch your mind. The bible said concerning Daniel that he was ten times better than others. He enjoyed that during his reign; in anything that was done, Daniel was preferred over others. There is an oil that makes you preferred over others! After sometimes, so many things came up and he was sacked and guess you who replaced him? The young lady!

I like you to build enough confidence against evil, against

hatred, against unrighteousness, against people who would want you to trade your destiny for something temporary and say 'No! I won't give it to you'. If they say you will not have it, then you can go your way. The bible says our afflictions in this life is for a little, build your confidence in God. *'Cast not away therefore because it a has a great recompense of reward' (Heb 10:35).* Your reward is coming, so keep holding on! There is enough room to build confidence in God and be successful in this world. There are scriptures that encourages us to build confidence in God so do not think that it is just all about speaking in tongues, it is relevant for everything in your life. The Holy ghost has the solution for everything, never mind the way people have portrayed the holy spirit in our dispensation as being for only miracles. He is completely more than a miracle; he is a way of life. The Holy spirit is about the way of life it is about everything if you carry him along, he is relevant for marriage, relevant for inspiration, relevant for business relevant for everything. In Psalms 139:14, what scripture says defines you and builds confidence in you, don't let your confidence be on what somebody has told you.

Do you know some people's mouth and heart may speak deception most times? Somebody says 'oh! you are looking so beautiful'. Do you know what he is saying in his heart? Don't build your life on what people say, appreciate what people say. When people compliment you, thank God and let it end there. Don't return home hallucinating on it. However, I know somebody who when He says 'you are looking good', means simply that. That's Jesus, if He says you are fine, you're fine. People lavish others with soothing words but afterwards their actions speak otherwise but I know one ancient of days that tells you 'I love you' and that love hasn't reduced, He says, 'Even in your sin I still love you'.

Know that you are wonderfully and fearfully made. Anybody who doesn't like you the way you are looking isn't meant for you, shift and move to another place. Love is unconditional, scriptures say while you were yet sinners, Christ died for you. God says you are fearfully and wonderfully made. Accept the validity of scripture, scripture says you are fearfully and wonderfully made so as you step out in the morning, you should tell yourself that. For as a man thinketh, so he is. Don't let your confidence be destroyed because of what somebody says. Somebody says that he wishes that you can be like someone–Don't accept such testimony. Building your confidence in God will help you succeed.

> *'Now unto him that is able to do exceedingly,*
> *abundantly above all that we may ask or think*
> *according to the power that worketh in us.'*
> *– Eph. 3:8*

This is attesting to the fact that your Father in heaven is able to do exceedingly and abundantly. Where is the power? In you! The problem is that you aren't using the power. God has placed something inside you to make you successful, do you know that? The prayer you should be praying is that God should open your eyes to see. Stop envying other people! There is enough power in you to make you become who God has ordained you to be, put it to work! God would not have made you a mistake and put something small in you that makes you look like a deficiency on the face of the earth. I was preaching in a pastors' meeting someday where I said to them to 'engage the oil'. There was a poor widow whose two sons were carried away because of poverty, hunger, lack and all manner of embarrassment. The woman had things in her heart, she kept claiming 'my husband served God, my husband feared God, my husband did this and that' as if God was owing her husband. Now the husband was dead. When the prophet asked her for what she had in her house, she said 'nothing!'. God cannot make you and leave you with nothing. 'You mean there is nothing?', the prophet said. She replied, 'well there is one small oil. If the oil was useful, how come we are in this condition? 'You mean you have oil in the house yet you are in debt? May God cause that which He has given to you to come alive in the name of Jesus! May Grace begin to open the door to nations for your potentials, your gifting, to find expression in the name of Jesus.

God cannot be wicked to have sent you to this world and not give you anything, He sent Moses on an assignment, while Moses complained, God showed him how that the rod in his hand was more than what he had taken it for. Do you know one of the problems is that God has given you something and you are underutilizing it? The rod is not just meant for taking care of the sheep, the rod is meant for signs and wonders. God told Moses to drop the rod in his hand and he saw how this rod turned to a snake. He stood surprised, God said to him to pick it up again, there is more to that which God has deposited in you.

You have the ability to control the manifestation of what is happening in your life. Moses picked it up. God said 'this is enough, go and meet Pharaoh with this'. You know that was the last thing that broke Pharaoh's back because after the Passover, they still pursued the Israelites. As Moses cried to the Lord, God told him that there was something in his hand and he had to use it. There is something in your life–my prayer is that the power of God, the breath of God will come upon what you have today in the name of Jesus Christ! Whether it is your voice, your certificate or your talent, the power of God will come upon it in the name of Jesus! You will no longer be small; you will no longer be looked down upon. All you need is the breath of God, once the breath of God, the blessing of God comes upon you, that's all! Don't say you don't have anything. Everybody is a carrier of God's deposit; that's why nobody should marry you out of pity.

A young man said to a lady 'I am marrying you so I can take away the shame of your family'. What an insult! Let nobody marry you out of pity. One of my daughters many years back came to me, she said 'this man said that after some time, if I don't say 'yes', he has seven other girls on the waiting list'. I told her go back and ask him which number she was because if she was the only one, he would wait. Otherwise, the day she will offend him, he will drive her away. There should be love, mutual love for people who want to marry. Don't sell yourself so cheap because you are from a poor family. The bible says who has despised the days of little beginning? Everybody has a little beginning; you can come from a poor family but don't let anybody look down so much on you to the point of molesting you.

God guarantees your journey in life–Job36:11 "If they obey and serve him, they shall spend their days in prosperity and their years be blessed." Things can be hard now but there is the promise of God, keep serving God. Nobody will serve him in vain–the bible says that anyone who seeks God must know that He is a rewarder of them that diligently seek him. You diligently seek Him and He will bless you. Don't let anybody deceive you, nobody has served God and became miserable. In Genesis 4, Abraham was well stricken in age, he was old and God had blessed him in all things! Things may be difficult at the moment but you must choose to build confidence in God. Tell yourself that in some few years to come, my story isn't going to remain the same.

What makes a man important in life is not his job, it is the favor of God. I knew that many years ago so I tried to behave myself well whenever I come before God. The book of Ecclesiastes says *'Time and chance happeneth to them all'.*

'But you are a chosen generation, a royal priesthood, an holy nation, a peculiar people that you should show forth the praise of him who has called you out of darkness to his marvelous light.'–1peter 2:9. This is a reflection on our identity; hence you must build confidence in God because it lasts longer. Don't build confidence on philosophical sayings, else, you keep reading some of those philosophical books until you end up with some of them who later committed suicide. Go around with the mindset that you are a royal priesthood; nobody can

challenge you.

Revelation 1:6 says He hath made us kings and priests unto our God and his Father to him be glory and dominion forever and ever. There is nothing wrong in confessing that you are a prince, go around with the correct identity. Don't let your present disposition determine your future disposition. Jesus was born in a manger but he didn't die in a manger; Jesus was born in a manger yet he isn't returning to a manger. You are permitted to start from anywhere because sometimes, you can't determine how you start. You don't determine where you are born, your birthplace can be near the market. You could even have been picked up from an orphanage, you can't decide that but you can decide with God, how your journey will go in life.

I am a very happy child of God. He says you are the apple of His eyes (Zechariah 2:8). Don't go about your life like an ordinary person, don't just dress in the morning without loading yourself with scriptures. You confess things like: 'God is my father, touch not my anointed and do my prophet no harm'. As you do this, you build confidence.

A young lady found herself in the midst of armed robbers after her bus was stopped and they were asked to surrender the money they had on them while those who didn't have money were killed. While all this went on, the lady said she didn't have money. They replied, 'you have everything we need.' After the first man tried to touch her, she burst into tongues out of fear, and then the man left her questioning why she would do such even while he hadn't touch her. Not quite long, they overheard vehicles passing by and took it to be the police; this made them run, leaving her and the other people. She had saved even the other people. Please, don't live an ordinary life, we are in the midst of extraordinary curriculum activities.

HOW DO YOU BUILD CONFIDENCE IN GOD?

- **Your Prayer life:** *'And this is the confidence that we have in him, that, if we ask anything according to his will, he heareth us'*–1 John 5:14. Your prayer life is very important. All your prayers shouldn't just be in the secret, do some prayers in the open for the sake of some wicked people. If you notice that thieves are always coming to your house, don't just pray secretly, rather get an anointing oil or water. Carry your oil, water or whatever you believe can work for you with your bible. Stay in front of your house and declare God's word as a siege over your territory. If you don't build confidence you can't do that!

The church I pastor has a land that came under heavy contention. On one morning, I went there and emptied a whole bottle of oil on the land and that contention was over. The papers were signed. Refuse to be too gentle.

- **The word of God:** *'This book of the Law shall not depart out of thy mouth but thou shall meditate therein day and day that thou mayest observe to do all that is written therein, for then thou shall make thy way prosperous* *and thou shall have good success'*–Joshua 1:8. Build your confidence in the word of God. Who told you that serving God will not make you successful? Success is not only measured in terms of money but in terms of how others are blessed through you coupled with how you make impact, then money will also come.

- **The Knowledge of Christ:** You can build confidence through your knowledge of Christ *(Col 1:27)*. *'To whom God would make known what is the riches of the glory of this mystery among the Gentiles; which is Christ in you, the hope of glory*. 1 John 4:4 also says Christ is in us. Say to the sickness, 'Christ is in me, this sickness can't live in me!' Christ means 'the anointed one'.

  'For I know the thoughts that I think towards you, saith the Lord, thoughts of peace, and not of evil, to give you an expected end.' Jeremiah 29:11.

God has plans for our lives. It doesn't matter what is happening now, I have experienced ups and down, some things do not go well sometimes. Excuse me, do you know that the fact you started a race as the first doesn't mean you will end first? It is not a guarantee, don't get too comparative in your thinking. God wants our attention because we are created uniquely. We are not in the same race at all, there are things that you will never touch now but when God opens the door, you will catch up and overtake. Don't get tensed by anything or anybody. God says, 'do you know what? I have plans for you'. Build confidence from what you know about God.

Know that all things have the ability to work for your good:

It doesn't matter what I face now, I know something–I am a child of God and I know that all things work together for my good. The bible says 'All things!' Do you know it will turn out for your good? The delay, accident will turn out for your good. Never joke with God–there are things people may not tell you from the bible; you will read the bible and think there were no accidents, no mishaps in the bible, there are! For some of those things, God made them good for these people. Ruth couldn't conceive, she was barren for ten years; she lost her husband not being able to bring forth a child but God turned it for her good. I don't know what your story is but God can turn it for good. God turned the story of Ruth for good, maybe there were people that were laughing at her; maybe there were some colleagues laughing at her. You keep saying, 'He has a son, I don't have a son.' Who do you compare yourself with? Ruth here didn't have a child, much worse was the fact that her husband was dead.

Have you ever been in a situation where people know about your past, they know what you have gone through, your challenges? Many people knew this woman's challenges. She was working one day in a farm and somebody came and said 'what! Look at this beautiful girl.' People kept murmuring, 'What is this man saying? Has he not heard her story?' 'Sir, maybe you didn't observe well, she is not a damsel, she's just Ruth, the Moabite', 'She married and couldn't bear a child after ten years, since her husband died, she's such a bad luck,' they exclaimed.

He said 'oh! this is the Ruth that followed Naomi back. Wow! Every time you are working, leave some portion for her and every time she needs help, render it to her.' He warned them sternly not to ever molest the woman. Rather the whole issue turning negative, since everybody knew her story, it was now becoming a gossip. Let people gossip your story, let them talk about what is not going well in your life, let them talk about what didn't do well in your life. What you need to do is to build confidence.

Ruth just followed Naomi's direction. The bible dedicates four chapters to this woman, Why? All things work together for good, thank God she didn't have a child because she would never have found her pathway. You must understand that our times are in his hands. God is turning what you think is bad around for your good in the name of Jesus Christ. Your faith must remain strong. *He staggered not at the promise of God through unbelief; but was strong in faith, giving glory to God' Rom 4:20.*

It is time to take your world, live your life to the fullest. Fulfill that dream and vision that God has given you. Don't let the past stop you, don't let people stop you, don't let whatever you have gone through stop you.

> *'Seek ye out of the book of the LORD, and read: no one of these shall fail, none shall want her mate:*

> *for my mouth it hath commanded, and his spirit it hath gathered them.*
>
> *And he hath cast the lot for them, and his hand hath divided it unto them by line: they shall possess it forever, from generation to generation shall they dwell therein.'–(Isa. 34:16–17)*

Do you have something that God has spoken to you about and you have abandoned? Dust the paper, remove it, start talking and praying about it–it is coming to pass. Lift up your eyes on high, stop looking down. *"…and behold who has created all these things, that bringest out their host by number: he calleth them all by names by the greatness of his might, for that he is strong in power and not one failest (Isaiah 40:26).* Go and live your vision!

Build confidence! Take your world! Live your life to the fullness! Remain unstoppable! Satan wants you to stop talking, he wants you to stop thinking, satan wants you to see things as impossible, your life is coming afresh in God. Never see any limitation in whatever God has laid upon your heart to do.

12

GRACE TO MOVE ON

*And we know that all things work together for
the good to them that love God and are called
according to His purpose.' (Rom. 8:28)*

GOD WANTS US TO KEEP moving, allowing nothing to hinder our flow with him. In 1 Samuel 16:1–3, God speaking to Samuel, said that Saul's season was over. There had been so much attachment between Samuel and Saul. Saul was the first physical king of Israel; God had always been their king but they said they preferred to have a king like other nations around. God in turn told Samuel to appoint unto them a king, so Saul became the first physical king, anointed by God. There were so many blessings that came Saul's way, at a time he functioned as a prophet, he prophesied to a point where people began to question 'Is Saul a prophet? 'There were divers testimonies and great happenings in the life of Saul. Sadly, a time came when Saul missed it. He became people–

conscious, he decided to please men rather than God. God gave him opportunities, yet he messed them up. At a point, God declared his era over, declaring another era open.

This is an era where the church is set to move into her next season. Saul was a privileged king but a time came when his season ended. God is a God of season; there are new seasons in the agenda that He wants us to step into. There are two deceptions that the devil poses that makes men not to step into new seasons of their life.

- **Good things of the past**

The first deception are the good things that you have experienced in the past season(s). It took God himself to condition that somebody be fired because He has opened another season for Him. Yet, because the man loves the previous season so much, he wouldn't want to quit the job. Meanwhile, in God, there are destinies that are waiting for his rising. Seeing now that he has been sacked, he would proceed to seek God. The same God that told the Israelites to go to Horeb where he encountered them was the same God that told them to get out of Horeb because they had stayed too long there.

Beautiful things may be happening at the moment and they might make you think you can't get something better than that. So, you are enjoying it, yet, God is not delighted about it. Don't enjoy what God is angry with, it is too dangerous. Don't stay where God has left—God told Samuel to stop crying because Saul's season was over.

Samuel was so much in love with Saul that even when God asked him to go to the house of Jesse, he was still looking for someone that looked like Saul. Sometimes, God is opening a new season for you but you are still thinking that it will look like the previous one. Some years ago, I heard of the story of a Nigerian footballer who was the best in his club, in fact the most valuable person in his club. People loved him so much until a coach discovered his skills and decided to take him out of the country to play. He then discovered that the season he was playing in Nigeria was not the same as now when he had to play outside the country, the season had changed. When your season changes, everything about your life will change.

- **Bad experiences of the past**

The second deception about change in season that may not allow people to move into their next season are the bad things that have happened in previous seasons of their lives. God might want you to learn something in a place for some certain years and then release you into another season but you might be blocking him because you are not enjoying the previous season. Every vision and assignment is tied to a time and season, there is no permanent season. When people continue to reflect on past disappointments, delays, betrayals, and all the bad things that have befell them, they remain in a season except they come into an understanding of the mind of God.

Joseph said to his brothers, 'don't be afraid my brethren, don't be angry or condemn yourselves, I will do you no evil. What you have planned for evil, God has turned it around for good.

Thank God you planned all those things against me, if you didn't plan to sell and lie against me, how would I have gotten to Egypt? How would I have fulfilled my destiny? How would I have been someone that will preserve a whole generation. Thank God you sold me out, thank God for your betrayal, thank God for the evil you did to me but thank God more for the plans He has for me. Imagine that Joseph's brothers didn't sell him out, what would he have become? Probably the most favourite child of his father, yet if his father had died, there might have been nothing to will to him and his brothers because of the famine. Those that bought houses and possessed lands sold everything just to survive.

There are things you may be glorying about people in this season that will not have relevance in the next season. The coat of many colours and other things that Joseph's brothers were envious about became so irrelevant in the next season because of the famine. The bible says that a man's greatest enemy are the people around him. Everything they did against joseph was working around for his good, imagine Joseph's season in Potiphar's house, assuming that he didn't experience those evil, his highest position would have been the chief of all the servant or the most senior servant. You don't have to get too emotionally depressed because of what you are going through today, don't get too angry about those that betray you today. If you are in the will of God, then they are working together speedily for your lifting. 'And we know that all things (not some things) work together for the good to them that love God and are called according to His purpose.' (Rom. 8:28)

The rich fool was looking so relaxed, thinking he has achieved, He said 'I will pull all this barn down and build another one' God appeared to him and called him 'the rich fool'. So, we see that both the good and the bad forces can keep you from entering a new phase. There is a season that might not carry all the benefits and excitements of the previous season. The order of David's ordination was to be different from Saul's. God told Samuel to tell anyone who questioned him that he was going to offer sacrifice to God, so as he went, everyone was afraid. That season was different from the other season, the new season for Samuel looks a little bit secretive, Samuel told Jesse to gather his children because God says there is a king amidst them. (1sam. 16:4–10) The season God is bringing you into may not even look like it is promising, there might not even seem like there's hope or blessing, yet God is bringing you to a new season. What gives a season its identity is because God has said it.

The new season of your life may come with a lot of trails but God is still in the business of opening the season for you, the next season may come with a lot of challenges. Your current season may not look like the season of abundance, the season may look challenging and scary but God is still in charge of your destiny. God said to prophet Samuel that there was still remaining somebody in Jesse's house that is yet to be given an opportunity. The season is not about what you have acquired but how much you know about God.

You may not look like the man of the season, David too didn't look like it, but surrounding David were great opportunities, forget about the good things you have enjoyed, forget about the bad things that have happened, all you need is for God to anoint you for every season.

13

GRACE FOR WISDOM

"Divine wisdom is the believer's advantage, it separates men. The problems of nations can be solved if divine wisdom is tapped into."

THAT WHICH GIVES DIRECTION TO power is called 'wisdom'. Divine wisdom comes from above, the bible says *'the wisdom from above is above all'* Remove wisdom from power, there can be a lot of problems. Power can kill, including that which is spiritual. There was a time in the bible when people would queue before Moses from morning to night and someone said 'this is not proper. 'Before this time, there were some people that came to tell Moses the same thing, but God afflicted them because they didn't apply wisdom, but someone else came and applied wisdom in giving Moses a counsel of wisdom and he followed his advice. Jethro, Moses' father–in–law counseled him to solve concrete issues and delegate some other people to solve lighter issues. Moses went to God and

He told him to go ahead.

POWER VERSUS WISDOM

We are in the days of power, but apart from power you need wisdom. We need wisdom because it is wisdom that creates light, solve unemployment problems, creates jobs and not power. The church in Nigeria has a lot of power, miracles are happening, signs and wonders are taking place but most people are living below average, it means that power alone is not enough, we need to apply divine wisdom to know how to control, manage, explore, create, invent, and take over. Opportunities can open up by power but you need wisdom to manage it, else you will get into problem or future doors close. Here are some highlights from scriptures that establish the superiority of wisdom over power;

> *'be not that envious against evil men neither desire to be with them' Wisdom will help you do a lot of things. Wisdom will keep multiplying all you have and it will keep opening more opportunities.–Prov 24:1–14*

'Then said I, Wisdom is better than strength nevertheless the poor man's wisdom is despised, and his words are not heard'– Ecclesiastes 9:16–17. You need to allow wisdom translate into things in your life.

When you don't apply wisdom, you labour yet you have nothing to show for it. (Ecclesiastes 10:10, 15) I can recollect the instance of one of the youths in our church that takes home lessons, he told me he was not making much money from it even though he was really putting so much effort into the work, this is where power is functional. I prayed for him that God would give him one or two lessons that will bring so much profit. Not so long, a highly placed person employed his service for his children. He was so wise not to ask for money from him; there is a lesson here—when money becomes your first principle of negotiation, you have failed. He didn't ask for money rather, he was just teaching the children. What he received in a month was so much that he was able to cover up for other lessons. Wisdom is profitable to direct so that you won't labour in vain.

It is better to go after wisdom than gold (Prov. 16:11,16); I tell people not to allow money be their priority when in search of a job because you can work in a place and acquire wisdom that will help you create something better than where you are working in a short time. In Acts 7:10; the bible talks about Joseph who had uncommon favour. Without wisdom, a man can land into trouble. By wisdom, Joseph became governor in Egypt, wisdom took him from the prison to the palace. (Gen 41:39–40) Pharaoh knew that Joseph was a non–indigene, this is just like the case in Northern Nigeria here because most of the times, people complain that we are not all Muslims but the power of wisdom breaks those limitations.

When people say that a problem cannot be solved, it is not true. Pharaoh ordered that the astrologers, magicians, and physicians be gathered. They might have even underrated Joseph's ability to interpret the dream. Pharaoh said to Joseph, 'what does my dream mean? 'Joseph replied, 'the seven fat cows means seven years of abundance, the seven fat corns means seven years of abundance. Also, the seven thin cows and corns means seven years of famine, a time will come that there will be surplus but another time will come that there will be famine and the years of famine will be so much that it will swallow the years of abundance up'. Pharaoh said 'yes, that is the interpretation! 'He then appointed Joseph as the one to handle the problem, regardless of whether he was an indigene or not.

What I am addressing here is the subject of divine wisdom— the ability to solve complex problems. Divine wisdom is a spirit, you don't learn it from school, you encounter it with God. Divine wisdom is the believer's advantage, it separates men. The problems of nations can be solved if divine wisdom is tapped into.

MEN WHO WALKED IN DIVINE WISDOM

DANIEL

Daniel 1:7 records that God gave Daniel favour and wisdom. It is not always your rank that makes the difference, it is the problem that you solve. Many years ago, I heard the story of an officer who was leading a team, they went for war and the casualties were too much. An elderly officer called him and said there was a young officer in their midst there who has the wisdom and capacity of a general even though he was not a general by rank. The captain sent for the young officer. He took him into his room, exchanged his uniform for the young officer's, and mandated him to wear the uniform while he, the captain, put on that of the younger officer. This left the young officer's colleagues in shock, he now had to take over the formation of the battle and everything changed in a jiffy. They didn't only kill the opponent, they re–possessed their city, and when it was time to give the honour, it was given to the captain. You would ask 'why?' It was because the captain displayed wisdom.

BEZALEEL

Another wonderful display of divine wisdom is found in the story of a young man, Bezaleel in Exodus 31:3, the bible talks about Bezaleel and some other children that God gave wisdom. I want you to know that God gives wisdom, the church needs to come to this reality if anything will change, we need to come to this phase. To have wisdom is to control, expand, explore and manage. Until we arrive at this standpoint, power alone will fail us and the church abased. There has to be a manifestation of wisdom, of Bezaleel, God said *'I have filled him with wisdom and understanding, knowledge and all manner of workmanship.* 'This is the advantage you have in your career, for whatever certificate, skill or training that you may claim to have undergone, others have it too. In fact, we have people that have gone through much more but your access into the realm of the spirit to tap divine wisdom makes the difference.

SOLOMON

Solomon went to God in 1 Kings 4:29 and God asked him what he wanted. 'Wisdom,' he said. He didn't even ask for money nor all the land of the philistine that his father was fighting for, he rather went for wisdom. 'I have stayed with my father I saw him mighty and very wealthy but I think I prefer wisdom', Solomon said. God gave Solomon what he has inquired–wisdom, understanding and a large heart even as the sand of the sea shore. You don't give what you don't have, so when you read in the bible that gold and silver was in abundance during the days of Solomon, it was because he had the capacity to turn his wisdom into wealth.

Are you into a business? Don't you think it can multiply and expand into an international business by divine wisdom? Are you pursuing a career? Do you know that divine wisdom can make your voice to be heard all over the world? Divine wisdom removes struggle from you, it also gives you an edge, location notwithstanding.

JESUS

Jesus, our perfect example, was already filled with wisdom right from the womb. (Luke 1:30–42). *'she spake out with a loud voice, and said, blessed art thou among women, and blessed is the fruit of your womb.'*–v. 42.

In Luke 2:52, the bible says that Jesus also increased in wisdom. At primary/basic school level, there is a level of wisdom you need, the same as when you are in secondary school/college. This is the same way you grow in life–you need to increase in wisdom. Isaiah 33:6 says *'wisdom shall be the stability of your time'*–when things are going upside down, you need wisdom. Wisdom equips you with the ability to know what to do even in the midst of crisis. In Gen. 26, there was famine in the land but what differentiated Isaac was divine wisdom.

> *'That I (wisdom) may cause those that love me to inherit substance; and I'll fill their treasures'–*
> *Proverbs 8:21*

WISDOM AND OUR RESPONSIBILITY

In Psalms 105:22, wisdom gives us an assignment, it's our responsibility to teach senators, this is why we keep praying that senators will arise from amidst the church. Ephesians 3:10 says that the church will demonstrate the manifold wisdom of God yet the church still finds it difficult to cope outside there. As soon as you step outside church, everything looks disorganized, the roads are bad, no water, no light, no security–these are all absence of wisdom. So as Christians, our demonstration of wisdom should not be limited to the church. Our mission should be to transform the society. The church is to demonstrate wisdom and not just miracles–after a man has been healed of a sickness, he needs wisdom to retain his healing because you need wisdom to live healthy. In as much as we are not ignorant of demonic forces, you need wisdom to live and multiply what is in your hands. As Christians, divine wisdom is our advantage.

Action point

The book of James says 'if you need wisdom, you should ask God'. Tell God to increase you in wisdom.

14

PREPARING FOR UNCOMMON FAVOUR

'Eyes have not yet seen, ears have not heard
neither has it entered into the heart of man,
what God has prepared for those that love him'.
(1 Cor. 2:9)

THERE'S A LEVEL OF FAVOUR that is not the usual favour that every child of God has; it is called uncommon favour. When you are born again, there is a level of favour deposited on you. It is possible you remain at that level of favour and not increase. The problem with a lot of people is not that God has not blessed them, rather they have not been able to grow it. This is where coming into an understanding of what God has given to you needs to grow.

'And the child grew, and waxed strong in spirit,
filled with wisdom: and the grace of God was

upon him.'–Luke2:40

From the passage above, you must have noticed that it was said the child grew and was filled with the wisdom of God, but in Luke2:52, it was recorded that Jesus increased in wisdom. Every phase of your life needs an increase in what God has deposited in you. The level of wisdom that Jesus needed as a child was not the same as the wisdom he needed as an adult, there must a growth process. In this light, Uncommon favour is the kind of favour that comes upon a person, changing such life forever regardless of tribe, colour and education or job. It changes your life completely. It brings you into God's fullness of manifestation. It doesn't happen all the time but when it comes, it comes to balance things in your life, it comes to bring comfort, it comes to fulfil what God has spoken over your life.

I will be showing you from the bible very soon those who enjoyed uncommon favour and why we need to prepare for it. Everyday of my life, I see things happening to people and I say, 'God, preparation is so vital!'. This uncommon favour is coming but we must be prepared for it. So, if Jesus increased in wisdom, in stature, and in favour with God and man, How about you? Don't think where you have come now is the best, you have not seen anything.

> *'Eyes have not yet seen, ears have not heard*
> *neither has it entered into the heart of man,*
> *what God has prepared for those that love him'.*
> *(1 Cor. 2:9)*

There should be a difference between those who serve God faithfully and those who don't. Indeed, this uncommon favour is coming to balance somethings in your life. For they that appear before God in Zion must move from one degree to another. They are not stagnant.

JOSEPH AS A CASE STUDY

Let's begin with the man called Joseph in whose life we see what uncommon favour can do, it takes a man out of prison. Don't be surprised when you hear prophetic words coming to your life about a shift that is set to happen. What you just have to do is believe and claim it because when uncommon favour locates you, it will make things work faster than you can imagine.

Joseph's master took him, and put him in prison, a place where the king's prisoners were bound: and he was there in the prison.

'But the Lord was with Joseph, and shewed him mercy, and gave him favour in the sight of the keeper of the prison. And the keeper of the prison committed to Joseph's hand all the prisoners that were in the prison; and whatsoever they did there, he was the doer of it. The keeper of the prison looked not to anything that was under his hand; because the Lord was with him, and that which he did, the Lord made it to prosper.'–
Genesis 39:20–23

Then Pharaoh sent and called Joseph, and they brought him hastily out of the dungeon: and he shaved himself, and changed his raiment, and came in unto Pharaoh. (Genesis 41:14)

Joseph, who was the same man that was in the prison in genesis 39:20–23 is that same man we read about in Genesis 41:14. I thank God that those who knew Joseph in prison were still alive. It is not all your enemies that must die. The bible says that God anoints my head with oil in the presence of my enemies and my cup runs over (Psalms 23:5). That means that not all your enemies will die, some of them will witness your greatness. In Genesis 41:14, Pharaoh sent for Joseph and they brought him out quickly out of the dungeon and he shaved himself and changed his raiment and came unto pharaoh. Stop running after things to look good, when favour comes upon you, it will show naturally. You don't have to kill yourself for any of those things–your season is coming. Your preparation is what is important. There was a need to prepare for the uncommon favour. Favour took Joseph out of the prison even when he least thought of it. For your faith to build an expectation towards God, don't think small, don't plan small! When favour comes, it will make all those things you are planning and praying for to come to pass.

DANIEL AS A CASE STUDY

Sometimes, we fail to believe prophecies that have gone out concerning us because of our present condition. One day, somebody told me, 'With all these things they are saying, how will it come to pass?'. Someone else walked up to me in the office and asked, 'all these prayers we keep rendering, when will it come to pass?' They have forgotten that faith is supposed to say *'be it done to me according to your word, according to your promises.'* We must remain prepared for uncommon favour.

To be prepared does not insinuate that you know when favour will come your way, rather, you are to do some of what God has spoken that you should be doing while waiting and it will come to pass. When uncommon favour comes, it will separate you from your friends, it will reduce so much labour that you are putting into life.

> *'For by strength shall no man prevail'; 'it is in vain for a man to rise early in the morning and sit up late in the night only to eat the bread of sorrow' (1 Sam 2:9, Psalms 127:2).*

Scriptures say *'lo he giveth his beloved sleep.'* If you think that the job you are doing is the best job because you earn money off it, you are making a big mistake. There are some people that are not doing that which you are doing but they are better than you, they have time to serve God. I have told God in my life not to give me anything that will not make me serve him in the name of being employed, not having time for God.

When people come to meet me, telling me that they got a job, the first thing I ask them is whether it will give them time to attend midweek services and Sunday service. I tell them to go and discuss with their boss and if their boss says 'No', I tell them to leave the job and look for another one. It is dangerous to work where you can't serve God, you won't last. The company itself may not last. I recognize the fact that sometimes, the temptations are much. I once told the story of one of our members who got a 100% scholarship including ticket fee but the source was questionable. She had passed the interview, wrote some papers and was selected but the conditions were not reasonable especially there are some places where you are not allowed to work anywhere except after when you worked with them first for some time. I told her to get her husband's advice on the scholarship; at last she missed the opportunity. After some months, another opportunity showed up. This time around, she called me from Kaduna informing me that she got a phone call, having a successful interview, this time around, it was a genuine one with 100 percent sponsorship.

Money is not everything – some people will look out for the one with the highest amount of money and go for it, claiming that 'heaven helps those who help themselves'. Daniel and his clique were ordinary children brought from captivity, they were like people that were taken out of war and brought up. In Dan 1:1–5, they were being trained, even though it looked like their destiny was under the influence of their circumstance, uncommon favour came upon them. These four were single-handedly selected because divine favour was upon them. The favour unleashed upon Daniel was not the same as for others, this is why uncommon favour will separate people. Even after few years in the land of Babylon, Daniel was recorded as being preferred above others.

Sometimes, people start to get jealous and angry for the way you are being respected, the way you are being called upon, they quickly forget that it is not your fault. Rather, what is happening to you is uncommon favour. There is just something so special about you. Daniel was preferred above the president and princes because an excellent spirit was on him and the king thought to set him over all of them. There are outstanding presidents among presidents there are presidents, even among Christians. For Daniel, uncommon favour separated Him so much that the king declared that he was different.

ESTHER AS A CASE STUDY

Esther was an orphan (Esther2:1); she was staying with Mordecai. She experienced the kind of favour that didn't happen to everybody in the bible. It comes upon certain people and change their lives forever, helping them to leave a lasting legacy throughout their generation. In those days, when the king was angry, Esther could walk into the presence of the king uninvited even when nobody could go in to see the king at such time. She told the Jews, 'pray for me, I will go all the same. If I perish, I perish.' When the king saw her, rather than condemning her, he stretched forth his scepter saying, 'Come! Whatever you want, even to a portion of my kingdom, I will give you'. Uncommon favour causes a person to appear in the days that things are not working well. Many organizations are closed down, many have lost their jobs globally, yet, many other organizations are raising people.

In the days of uncommon favour, people are losing their jobs but other people are getting a new job, heavyweight jobs. Uncommon favour made a whole lot of difference in the life of Esther.

RUTH AS A CASE STUDY

She was the Moabite who had a questionable background and a great story (Ruth 1:4). Deut. 23:3 She experienced ten years of bareness, ten years of nothing. Eventually, her husband died; then in Ruth 4:10–13, things began to work in her favour. Uncommon favour came upon a stranger, Ruth. Her surname changed in verse 10. An encounter that takes away the shame of a person, the day Boaz took Ruth as wife, she ceased to be called a 'Moabite', when he went in unto her, the same woman that couldn't give birth. Where you put your head matters a lot. Whether you are successful or not depends on what you know about God. The same woman that couldn't give birth for ten years now conceives; the Lord granted her uncommon favour. The woman told Naomi, *'Blessed be the Lord which has not left you this day without a kinsman and that his name be famous in Israel and he shall be unto day a restorer of thy life'* (Ruth 4:14–15)

NEHEMIAH AS A CASE STUDY

Uncommon favour helps a man to recover, taking people from one realm to another. It can take a man from one dimension of grace to another. Nehemiah was in the palace as a cupbearer, he was a man given to God's service. Anywhere you are working and your Christianity cannot show forth, it is not a good place to work. He was praying and fasting unto God, after sometime in Nehemiah 2:12, he made himself available for the problem to be solved until he finished the work. This same cupbearer now becomes a governor because of uncommon favour. (Neh. 5:14)

WHAT ARE WE TO LEARN FROM THESE LIVES?

- **Nehemiah**

The place of kingdom service is notable in the life of Nehemiah. It is good that you are concerned about what happens in the society but it is better that you are concerned about the kingdom. He heard about the shame and reproach that has come upon God's people because of the broken walls of Jerusalem. He told his boss that he needed to be involved in the course. He told himself, 'Our church is involved in carrying the burden of this nation, I need to be involved. Although, I can choose to enjoy the pleasures in the palace. 'Don't reduce your life to your present disposition, else you won't go far. He was not forced for service, he was told about the issue and it became a burden for him, he even fasted and prayed. He gathered like–minded men, understanding that what has brought him is kingdom service. Over the years I have availed myself the little opportunity I am given to serve. Yes, I engage in a lot of voluntary services yet it doesn't take the place of kingdom service. For anything that relates to the kingdom, I am available! God doesn't forget our service. Many years ago, I arranged computer classes for pastors even with my little knowledge. I did that for them to learn a little about the computer. Do whatsoever you can do, little resources you can render for the kingdom. God will always bless you in the seed that you sow, others will follow. In what you sow, the seed comes from there. God does not work by coincidence; he knows the end from the beginning. Sometimes, when money is not involved, some people don't like to serve. Live for service, not money.

When you engage in Kingdom service, do it with all your energy because as you do such, you are preparing yourself for uncommon favour. I met somebody sometimes ago from Tunisia who asked me to design content for them while I was appointed as a trainer. I had met him just once during a training on zoom. Doors open without begging for it as you serve some people. Some of the kingdom services are not even recognized by people but God sees your service, please find a place to serve.

•　Ruth

We learn good followership from Ruth. She was a good and diligent follower of instructions. I hope you knew that they were two people; two sisters were there. They took a decision to follow their mother–in–law back home after she lost her sons to whom the duo was married to. 'Even if I have another child now, you can't wait to marry him. 'One of them said 'No

'Something in her convinced her to follow this woman. Did you hear the terms of her commitment? *'where you go, I will go, where you live, I will live, what you eat I will eat, where you die, I will die, who you serve I will serve.* 'She was a follower of instructions.

Uncommon favour cannot come upon you when you break every instruction and you just keep praying. I once told someone that you cannot be an instruction breaker and not be 'a caster of demons. 'The Bible says, 'to obey is better than sacrifice, for rebellion is as the sin of witchcraft…' (1 Sam. 15:22, 23). You can't go far living a life of disobedience.

By the time they got to their town, Ruth's mother–in–law said, 'follow me and listen to my instructions, when you got to the farm', she said 'do this. When you see this man called Boaz, you act this way' Ruth replied, 'yes ma'. She was a follower of instruction. She got married to the wealthiest man in the city, immediately she took in, she gave birth. That woman was a Moabite, she was not supposed to even return let alone marrying. Your past is not as important as the decision you make today for your present.

•   **Esther**

We learnt the ability to be mentored from the life of Esther, the quality of being teachable. Esther had no parents and she lived with Mordecai. Mordecai said 'follow me, Esther' she said, 'yes sir' 'what I tell you, you will do just that,' she said, 'yes sir'. Esther could have resisted, claiming that she doesn't want her life to be controlled since she had her life to live. Mentoring is not about controlling one's life; it is giving direction because of something you don't know that others know. She was under the mentorship of Mordecai and she found her way to the palace. The enemies tried to eliminate the Jews but they couldn't because of every attack, she will take it back to Mordecai. I was thinking that now that she was in the palace, she would have forgotten the one who mentored her.

Many people forget their spiritual fathers and pastors, they claim not to need anybody to control them. This was not so for Esther; she was always going back to Mordecai. Even when there was trouble, Mordecai could offer the right counsel. Mordecai said, 'you have to go and see the king; go! we are going to pray for you. Who knows if it was because of a time like this that God has sent you here' and she said 'Alright, I will go.' Mordecai said 'if you don't want to go, God will raise help from another place; it is you and your household that will perish.' She said, 'I will go, I am still your daughter. That I am the wife to the richest man in the world doesn't make me your mother, I am still your daughter.' It is not about your age neither is it about your position. The whole Jewish race was preserved under the ministry of Esther through the guidance of Mordecai. Learn to listen! The road of a proud man or woman heads towards destruction. When you see someone who keeps resisting mentoring, find out what they have achieved that they don't want someone to control. Nothing! Every great man has someone that talks to him.

- ### Daniel

We learn the importance of diligence from Daniel. (Dan. 6:2) Daniel had a spirit of excellence, he was always doing his job well. Excellence is a good spirit. In whatever you do, do it like God. God is called the alpha and omega; you have got to start and finish it well. It is not enough to start and scatter it.

Daniel was preferred above all the young princes from Israel because he has an excellent spirit (Dan. 6:3). Let your presence bring positive impact. If you sing, sing well. Sing like your life depends on it; in whatever you are doing, give it your best. You are preparing for an uncommon favour. Don't do what you do because somebody is there to inspect, just do it well! Your boss doesn't have your reward, God does. You need not wait for commendation from anybody.

- ### Joseph

Joseph showed us the need to polish one's gift. Paul, speaking to Timothy said, *'stir up the gifts inside of you which you got by the laying on of hands by the presbytery.'* You may be like a cup or tin that has sugar beneath but because you have refused to stir up your gifts (put it to work), things seem not to work. There is something that you don't understand but you can learn more about. When favour comes it is usually to the proportion of what you have sown, you can't reap above what you have sown. So, polish that gift. The passion I expend when I preach the word of God stems from my preparation for Sunday services, I hardly sleep. Stir up your gifts and put it to work. Remember, the gift of a man will make room for him. Don't wait until you are called for rehearsals; do rehearsals in your room too, add prayers because prayer will bring impact.

As you prepare for the uncommon favour, ensure that you don't make the mistake of Saul, Samuel and David. Saul became proud, he was a nobody–the first king of Israel. Never let what God has given you make you proud. Saul became proud, someone who became a prophet without calling, sat down and honour was placed on him, he that wasn't planning to be a king but was just searching for his father's missing animal yet was anointed as a king. This same Saul became people–conscious, he cared more about how he appeared to the people. Samuel said, 'is it about people or God.'

It baffles me so much why Samuel made a similar mistake like that of Eli. Eli didn't wrong God rather, his children did. Eli's children set God against their father. God was angry with Eli because he was handling the affairs of his children with a light hand. The misbehaving children made for his doom. When they broke the news of his Children's death to him, he fell and died. Unfortunately, Samuel's children did worse, and God said 'Why? For this same reason, I brought you to replace Eli' Samuel's children were sleeping with women inside the church. God, testifying about Abraham, said 'For I know Abraham, he will command his children after him.' If you have a parent that tailors you, you'd better thank God; most parents don't have the time. It is anointing when a child wears his father's cloth, the anointing will rest on such child. You can choose to wear the anointing that keeps you alive or choose to wear fashion that cuts off your head. It is better to prepare for uncommon favour. Let's not make the mistake of David, Samuel, Saul or the rich fool. For the rich fool, it was money. 'Nobody should control what I do with my money, I decide whether I pay tithe or offering,' he said. God said 'you are a fool, this night, your life will be required of you. 'Only fools talk like the rich man did, the rich fool didn't lie against God nor did he steal. The way he was planning to spend the money made God call him a fool.

In conclusion, three things are important:

1.   Build capacity before uncommon favour comes upon you. When you don't have enough capacity, there might be a problem. David was not planning to be king, but when he became king. At the time he ought to go for a war, what he had fail to build capacity for brought pain to his generation. While he stayed at home, he was taken off by the sight of a naked woman who was taking her bath.

2.   Begin to sow seed; you sow because you are expecting favour. For instance, there are people in our local church who give to missions every month, and those same people give me money every month consistently for the past six years no matter how small it is. There are seed you should 'sow up' so that you can go up, there are seeds you sow down to the needy. If your seeds are always going down all your life, going up might be a little bit difficult for you.

3.   Back up your seed with prayers; you are set for uncommon favour.

15

ANOTHER CHANCE

ONE AFTERNOON, AS I SAT to meditate, I heard God ringing these words in my ears *'Lord, give me another chance.'* That's not a word to be taken lightly, to say 'another chance' means there was a chance that was either not utilized well, not necessarily that you messed up the chance. While there are those who mess up the chances and opportunities God gave to them, there are those who didn't utilize it well. These were those that were meant to reach fifty but stopped at twenty, some were meant to reach hundred they stopped at fifty yet they were rejoicing and comparing themselves with other people saying 'that guy stopped at twenty, I got to fifty 'but God says 'No, his own is fifty while yours is hundred'. Sometimes, God has given you opportunities yet you are saying 'Lord, give me another chance'. Let's consider two case studies from the bible, the first is found in *'Then Jonah prayed unto the Lord God.'–Jonah 2:1*

'And the word of the LORD came unto Jonah the second time, saying, Arise, go unto Nineveh, that great city, and preach unto it the preaching that I bid thee. So Jonah arose, and went unto Nineveh, according to the word of the LORD. Now Nineveh was an exceeding great city of three days' journey. And Jonah began to enter into the city a day's journey, and he cried, and said, Yet forty days, and Nineveh shall be overthrown.' Jonah 3:1–4(KJV)

'Then went Samson to Gaza, and saw there a Harlot, and went in unto her'–Judges 16:1

'And Samson took hold of the two middle pillars upon which the house stood, and on which it was borne up, of the one with his right hand, and of the other with his left. And Samson said, Let me die with the Philistines. And he bowed himself with [all his] might; and the house fell upon the lords, and upon all the people that [were] therein. So the dead which he slew at his death were more than [they] which he slew in his life.'–Judges 16:29–30(KJV)

We are not praying to die with our enemies like Samson did. It was Samson that prayed that prayer, but consider it from this angle, God may be speaking to a lot of people who have lost chances from reckless living, reckless decision, reckless perception or from things that didn't go well. Look at the way Samson was playing here, wow! Samson, the anointed of God, was playing with a woman. Women are powerful and graced; God has created beautiful things but you must know how to manage your life with women or you are gone forever. A woman must also know how to manage her life with a man, else you are gone–it's bi-directional. This 'Delilah' is a spirit; it can be a man or a woman because men do the same thing.

The greatest challenge of our time and the biggest problem in the world today is sexual sin. That's why rape is on the increase. People have become monsters in their imagination about sex, about women, about men–monsters! Samson was the anointed of God; his mission was okay but somewhere along the line he became careless, he was derailed. The devil took his attention and was going after his life. Sometimes In life, as we journey, we derail, sometimes in life we listen to bad advice, we make errors, sometimes we read wrong things. Sometimes I see people reading some books and I get scared because such book will lead them to taking a wrong decision. What you read is powerful, what you watch is powerful, what you think is powerful.

> *'God is able to do exceedingly, abundantly, above all that you may ask or think according to power that worketh in us.'–Ephesians 3:20*

It is very important we understand the power of asking but we need to also understand the power of thinking. Samson just missed the trap God had set for him; he became reckless in his living. He thought it was a joke, it started with *'if you*

tie me, I will be loosed the first time, second time third time' and he still continued like that. Some people have misused opportunities God gave them; some have messed up platforms God gave them. Sometimes back, I used to know of somebody who God gave another opportunity. Along the line, he became pressed and came under pressure by his family. Due to this, he started stealing; he stole until he was handcuffed and taken behind bars. When he was asked what went wrong, he said his family–family pressure. So, the family was called upon and quizzed thus; 'how many are you in the family?'. He had one wife, two children that are not up to ten years old, then where is the family pressure? The wife, giving her own response said, 'we are the only one that looks like we aren't doing well', so there was a comparison somewhere.

The bible says they that compare themselves with themselves are not wise! The pressure pushed the man into stealing. By the time he was eventually released after about ten years, his wife had left. All the eyes of the wife could picture was money! money! money!–just anything that could translate into money. Within ten years she had left, she had given birth to another two children for another man. While the man was still in prison, in the first year she was going to give him food like a faithful wife, even in the second year and third year; then one day she thought, 'This man is not coming out again.' After the man was released, he began his life afresh by looking for a church which he started attending. At a point, some people began to dissect his life, proclaiming that he was an ex–convict; some of these people who were gossiping were inside the church. The church where he should find help gossiped him but he had found the savior, Jesus right inside the prison.

While he was not yet a convict, he just went to church as a religious person. You know there are many religious people in church who look like Christian but they are perpetual Judas in the actual sense. They have different titles but have never met with Jesus; this man met Jesus in the prison. Now that there is nowhere to go, he was ready to focus on reading the bible. He became a better Christian; it was not a good experience but the bible says *'all things work together for good for they that love him and are called according to his purpose'*. He started praying, asking God to give him another chance. Who will give an ex–convict a chance? For all the places he went to look for work, once they went through his profile, they would commend him but promise to get back to him. Upon findings, once they discover he is an ex–convict, they just told him 'sorry this company does not take ex–convicts'. He spent years looking for work since nobody will want to employ an ex–convict.

He kept praying 'Lord, give me another chance'. He wasn't running away from the fact that he messed up. You know there are different categories of people:

- **The generation of Saul:** these ones have done what is wrong but they are not bothered.
- **The generation of David:** these ones don't care about who is there watching them like Saul who is bothered about such.

'Is there anyone that wants to give his life to Christ?' Saul looks out, as soon as he sees one of his lieutenants, he tells himself 'I can't mess up myself', then he remains on his seat, preferring to rotten in sin. For David, he lies down and says 'Oh God, have mercy on me'; he was a man that enjoyed another chance.

This man kept praying that the Lord will give him another chance; he was committed, he was doing fine of course. After he had seen his wife, he just went to have his children back to himself. Nobody was trying to find out why he went to jail including family members and in–laws, no one wants to associate with an ex–convict. He was no longer important; he was trying to please his family. When you earn up to five thousand naira (#500,0000) in a month, you can afford a cloth worth twenty thousand naira (#20,000) for a year–old but if you earn fifty thousand (#50,000) or a hundred thousand (#100,000) in a month and you buy a cloth worth forty–five thousand (#45,000) for a child, then it was all pressure and competition that landed him in prison. The people for which reason he was doing it all left him and here is he asking God to give him another chance.

On a certain day God told him, 'I will give you another chance'. He was thinking it was going to be a Job, all God gave him was an idea, and that small idea was to nurture people who had a similar problem like his. A seed gives birth to another seed; it is from a seed that you get harvest. God gave him an idea; he began nursing and nurturing it. He planted the idea and it started growing. Within years, the idea had blossom and became a household name. That was how this man started rising again, he was no longer somebody that needed to be employed; he could now employ people. In the space of ten years, he had over a thousand (1000) people he was paying salary, his life had become better, he was a better man. When you see him stepping out of his car, you will swear that this man was never poor because he lives with simplicity. Now, there is no pressure anybody can put on him; he is a very simple man but he is a multimillionaire. He spends his money in pushing forth the gospel and helping ex–convicts, establishing businesses for them. God has given him another chance, even though he missed it somewhere, even though he was reckless somewhere yet, God gave him another chance.

God is ready to give people another chance if only we will confess and say:

> *'Lord, we are sorry for that one. I was careless, I shouldn't have listened to that person, I shouldn't have followed what that person said, I got into this trouble by following the leading of this person, I got into this trouble by reading this kind of book. Now I need another chance'*

Indeed, God gave that man another chance. He has now become someone that can share his testimony with another, someone whose testimony encourages others. For Samson, he missed it, he was reckless with his life. Samson was anointed but he went after a harlot and the enemies got hold of him. They took Samson, mocked his life and his God, they removed his eyes and turned him into an entertainer. There are many destinies that lack direction, their spiritual foresight has been removed. Samson's life was brought to a halt; his life became a ridicule among men. He whose name alone could make people to run for fear now became an object of laughter. However, the bible said his hair started growing. Even though his hair grew, the power wasn't released because the power was not in the hair, the power is in the God that places it on the hair. So, while it was growing again Samson cried to God for another chance.

Your own may not be a reckless life of sin like Samson's, yours may not be like Jonah's who was sent on an assignment but he insisted to go his own direction. God said, 'since you want to choose your way, whatever you see is an affliction you brought upon yourself. The bible says that a whale swallowed Jonah for three days but when Jonah came back to his senses, he asked God for another chance and the whale vomited him, then Jonah went to Nineveh. So, yours could be the place of assignment, yours could be a business opportunity God gave you that somehow you destroyed, you were not diligent enough to nurture it to the next phase and it has all gone. Yours may be that you have come under attack–Isaac came under the attack of the philistines, they took his wealth, all that God promised him but God gave him another chance. Our directions may be different but everyone from time to time needs a second chance. God is saying, 'I am going to give you another chance.

Prayer: Lord, I had an opportunity but somewhere I lost it. Please, give me another chance.

16

GRACE FOR JOY

'Now the God of hope fill you with all joy and peace in believing, that ye may abound in hope, through the power of the holy ghost' (Romans 15:13)

To HAVE JOY IS TO know God and his promises. When joy is tampered with, your life is tampered with. It takes joy to even be a believer. There's still hope that things will get better, that's why we preach, pray, and talk like this. It is impossible to believe what scriptures say without joy. The bible says that *'hope maketh not ashamed...' (Rom. 5:5)*. It is very important that we keep hope alive, in whatever you are trusting God for, keep hope alive–the way to keep hope alive is to be joyful. Being joyful is not being happy, happiness is conditioned by means of happenings around, joy is produced from the inside. We derive joy from the knowledge of God and his promises, not just from knowing God alone because there are people that know God and are ignorant of his promises. Joy is derived from knowing God and his promises. His promises are 'yes and amen'.

The authenticity in the truth of God's word defies the reality of your current situation. It doesn't matter what you are seeing now, the word of God remains the same. You need joy to keep believing. Once joy leaves, your life and your Christianity start depreciating and you begin to doubt God. You must choose to believe God's promises towards you–you tell yourself, 'these are the promises of God to me, I believe his promise on healing, prosperity, protection 'In psalms 91, he said 'I will give my angels charge over you', 'No weapon formed against thee shall prosper' (Isaiah 54:17), it is God's promise and I believe it. My joy is not in those things I have acquired, it is in the promises of God.

> *'But thou shall remember the lord your God: for*
> *it is he that giveth thee power to get wealth...'*
> *(Deut. 8:18)*

I have victory because the word of God says so. Col 2:15 says ***And having spoiled principalities and powers, he made a shew of them openly, triumphing over them in it*** Refuse to make your possessions the source of your joy, it should rather be on God's promises. Then will you experience quality joy. Even the bible guarantees that there is fulness of joy in God's presence. Psalms 16:11

A man going through difficult and turbulent times who find

his way into God's presence will derive joy from God. A man returns from work and shouts 'hallelujah!', the wife run to him and inquires, 'Have you been promoted at your place of work' and he answers 'no, I was just sacked at my place of work', 'Why the hallelujah?' she asks 'because the lord reigns', the man echoes. God marks your comments, statements when things are not going on well with you. God is giving you something better, if He was not planning such, how come you lost that one. You have the promise of something better because you are a child of God, you have followed the covenant, you are a tither, you are a giver.

In Proverbs 17:22, the bible talks about joy like medicine–'A merry heart doeth good like a medicine...' When joy is coming from the heart it is very difficult to be sick. There's a great link between a heart that is full of joy and sound health. Medically, when a man starts getting depressed, he falls sick easily, your immune system starts collapsing when you are not just happy. Have you ever wondered why people still engage in the consumption of alcoholic drinks and prostitution despite its increase by 100%? It is because people assume that those things makes them happy at least for sometimes but they forget that real joy comes from God, the knowledge of God and his promises. When you know scriptures that propel your joy, they well up in you when situations come–'all things are working together for my good', 'for I know the thought I have towards you, it is of good and not of evil, to give you an expected end'. Be responsible for your joy, let your joy be tied to the kingdom.

'For the kingdom of God is not meat and drink; but righteousness, and peace, and joy in the Holy Ghost.' (Rom. 14:17)

Belonging to a kingdom like this, having a church where you are cared for and constantly being told the truth is part of what brings your joy, there is joy in the kingdom. We look towards joy in the midst of crises with the knowledge that 'weeping may endure for the night but joy comes in the morning', you just know that God is in control.

PRACTICAL STEPS TO WALKING IN JOY

Some people wonder why I am always joyful, they think it is because I don't have problems and I tell them, 'your own problems are also mine but I don't have to always put it on my head'. A child of God that has the holy ghost and is fully operating in it is better than a professor without the holy ghost—a professor is intellectually limited, a child of God with the holy ghost is unlimited. (1 John 2:7) Let me walk you through some steps to take in order to walk and abound in joy:

1.   **Feed on God's word:** In the midst of all unpalatable situations, it is right to feed on God's word. Joy is tied to what you hear because faith comes by hearing, John 15:11 says, ***These things have I spoken unto you, that my joy might remain in you, and that your joy might be full.*** That you are living in bitterness and strife is conditioned by what you are hearing, Jesus told his

disciples, 'you have joy by my word.' Sensor what you hear, hear the right things so as to balance your life.

2. **Understand that God made all things beautiful:** Psalm118:24 says 'This is the day which the Lord has made; we will rejoice and be glad in it 'Say it as many times as you can. Satan doesn't make any day; nobody can make your day except God.

3. **Know that joy comes only from God:** You have to register this in the depth of your heart that joy comes from the Lord and not material things (Psalms 4:7). Sometimes we find ourselves in what we did not plan for and God says 'keep hope alive, you are coming out of it strong'

4. **Keep hope alive:** You need to sustain a living hope, knowing that tomorrow will be better. (Prov. 4:18) Don't let anything weary you, don't let anything put tension on you. There is nothing as 'best' in the kingdom, we are meant to complement each other. Don't put unnecessary pressure on your life, your destiny is unique and different, don't equate yourself with someone else. Scriptures say that the path of the righteous is like a shining light that shines brighter and brighter (Prov 4:18). Indeed, 'the glory of the latter house shall be greater than the former.'

If you are a child of God, things will eventually work for you. You might have suffered loss or crises, keep hope alive that things will work for you. That someone started before doesn't mean the person will succeed before you, so as you wake every day declare that 'this is the day that the lord has made, I rejoice and I am glad in it.' The bible says 'he makes everything beautiful in its own time.' There are somethings that will come as gift to you in life, when God says 'he will supply all your need' he didn't say 'how'. You will get some while some will be given to you directly by God. Grace can pay the gift of a man and you can begin to live by grace, having your bills paid by grace. We put our trust in him when we know he is responsible for our joy. (Psalm 5:11)

The way life operates attests to the truth that ***the race is not to the swift and the battle is not to the strong but time and chances happeneth to them all***. Don't bring yourself under comparison. Wait, let God supply all your need. We live per phase and per time, and life will always improve for a child of God. Be careful about people who kill your joy with harmful words, may God separate you from them in the name of Jesus. The bible says 'mark them that cause division and throw them out of the church.' Be joyful and don't bother about what people say, fix you heart on God and keep your hope alive.